CONTENTS

Encouraging Interest
Help students to develop an understanding and appreciation for different artists and types of art by highlighting a variety of artists each month. Display examples of an artist's work and have students study and duplicate the style. In addition, encourage students to visit art museums online or visit local art galleries.

Student Sketchbook Ideas
Give each student a large sketchbook in which to explore art techniques, create designs, collect examples of artwork they admire and challenge their thinking about art. Encourage students to add to their sketchbooks at least once a week.

Coloring Pages
These pages are intended to give students practice in using different elements of design.

Rubrics and Checklists
Use the rubrics in this book to assess student learning.

Learning Logs
In addition to a sketchbook have students keep a learning log as an effective way to organize their thoughts and ideas about art concepts presented. Learning logs can include the following kinds of entries:
- teacher journal prompts
- questions that arise
- labeled diagrams
- student personal reflections
- connections discovered

Art Glossary
List new art vocabulary and their meanings on chart paper for students' reference during activities.

Elements of Design: Color Activities 2	Working with Elements of Design 47
Elements of Design: Value Activities 8	Discussion Prompts: Looking at a Painting 59
Elements of Design: Line Activities 12	Artist-Inspired Art Ideas 60
Elements of Design: Form Activities 18	Similarities and Differences 65
Elements of Design: Texture Activities 23	Direct Draw 66
Elements of Design: Space Activities 32	Sketchbook Drawing Ideas 67
Elements of Design: Shape Activities 35	Seasonal Art Ideas 68
	Art Rubrics 72
	Art Web Sites for Students 76
	Art Glossary 77
	Student Art Certificates 80

THE COLOR WHEEL

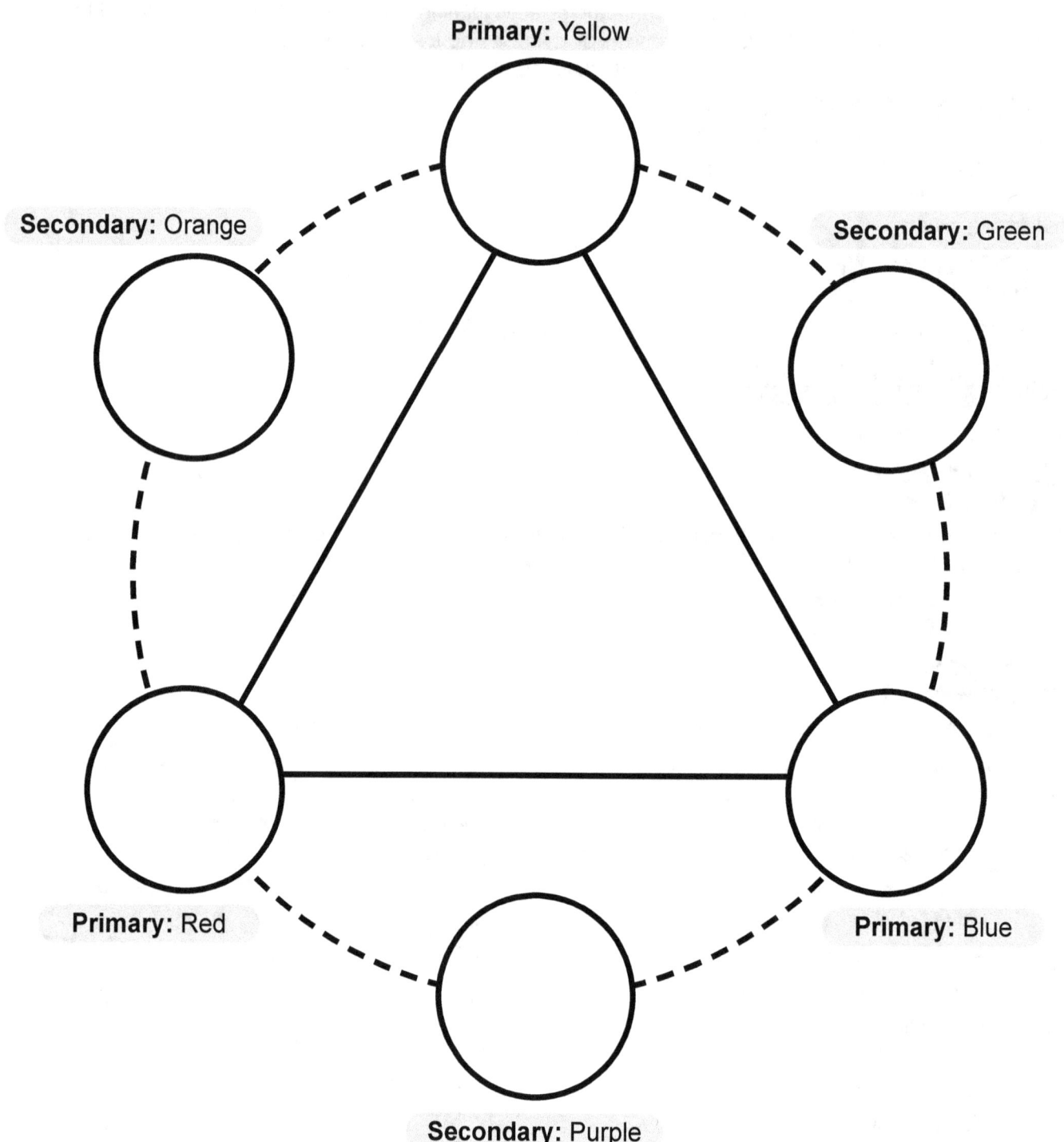

The **primary colors** are red, yellow and blue. Primary colors cannot be mixed or created by any combination of other colors.

The **secondary colors** are purple, green and orange. These colors are created by mixing the primary colors.

MIXING COLORS

What are the primary colors?

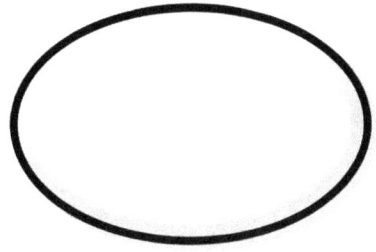 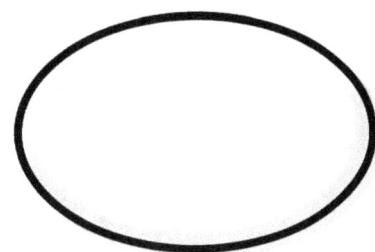 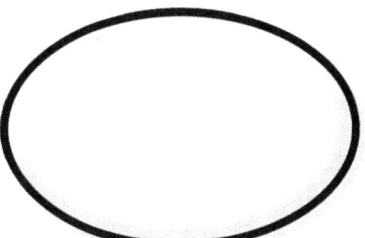

_____   _____   _____

Which primary colors make the secondary colors?

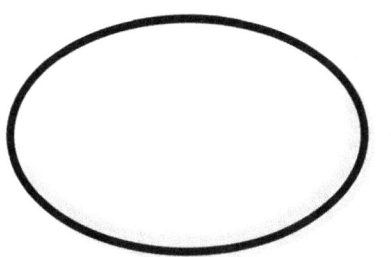 + 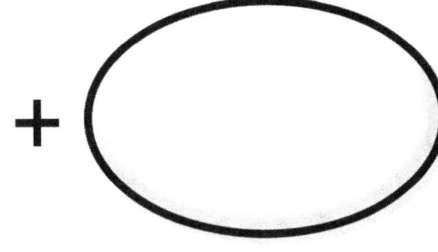 =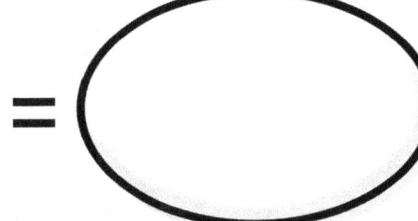

_____   _____   _____

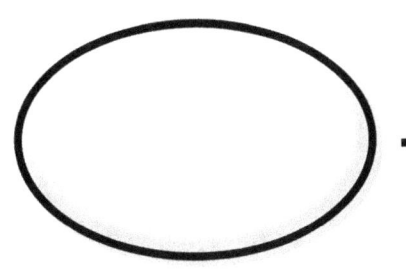 + ⬯ = ⬯

_____   _____   _____

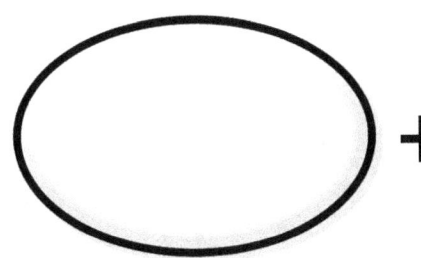 + ⬯ = ⬯

_____   _____   _____

COLORING FUN

Color the picture using only primary colors. Make sure to color in the background.

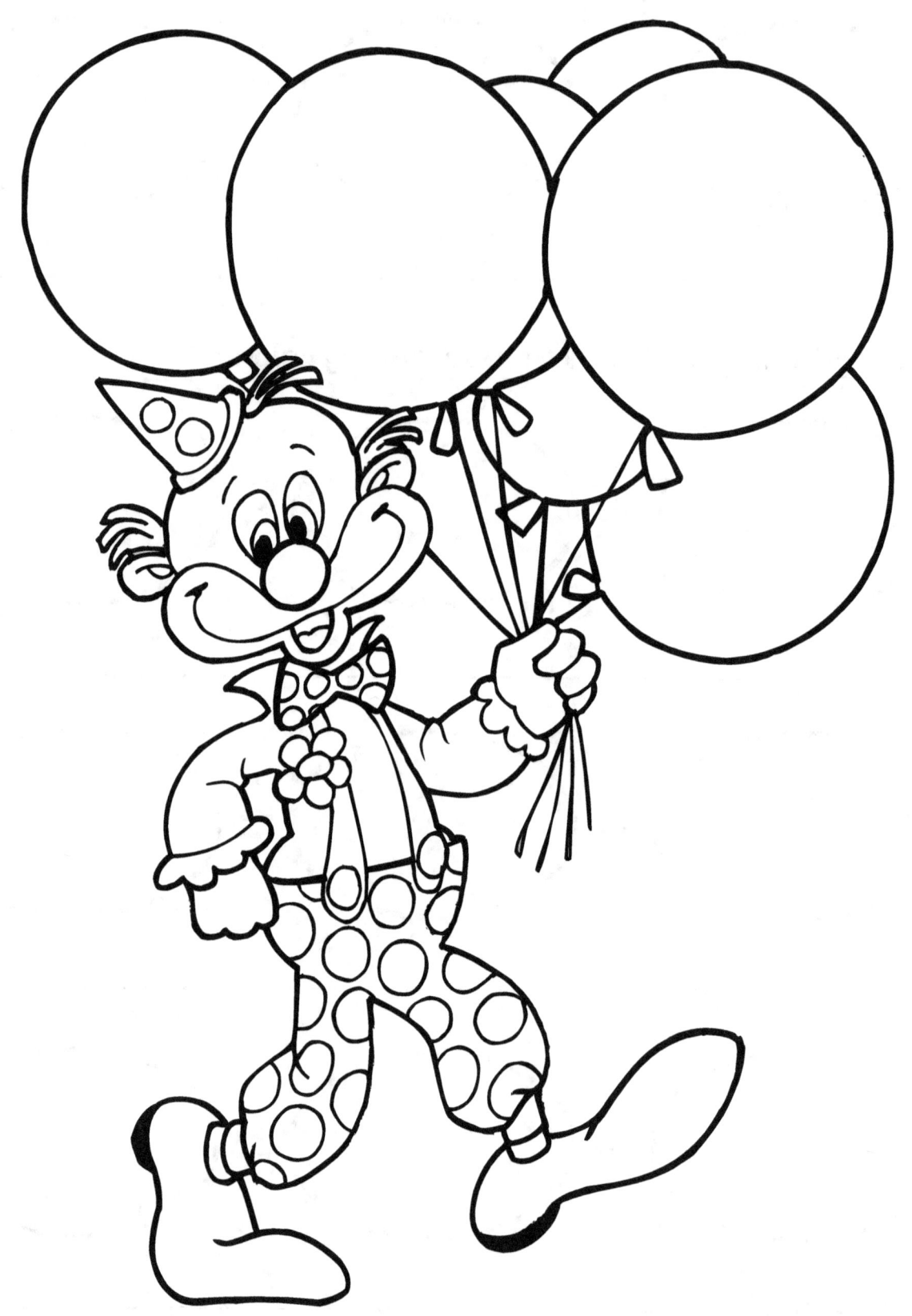

COLORING FUN

Color the picture using only secondary colors. Make sure to color in the background.

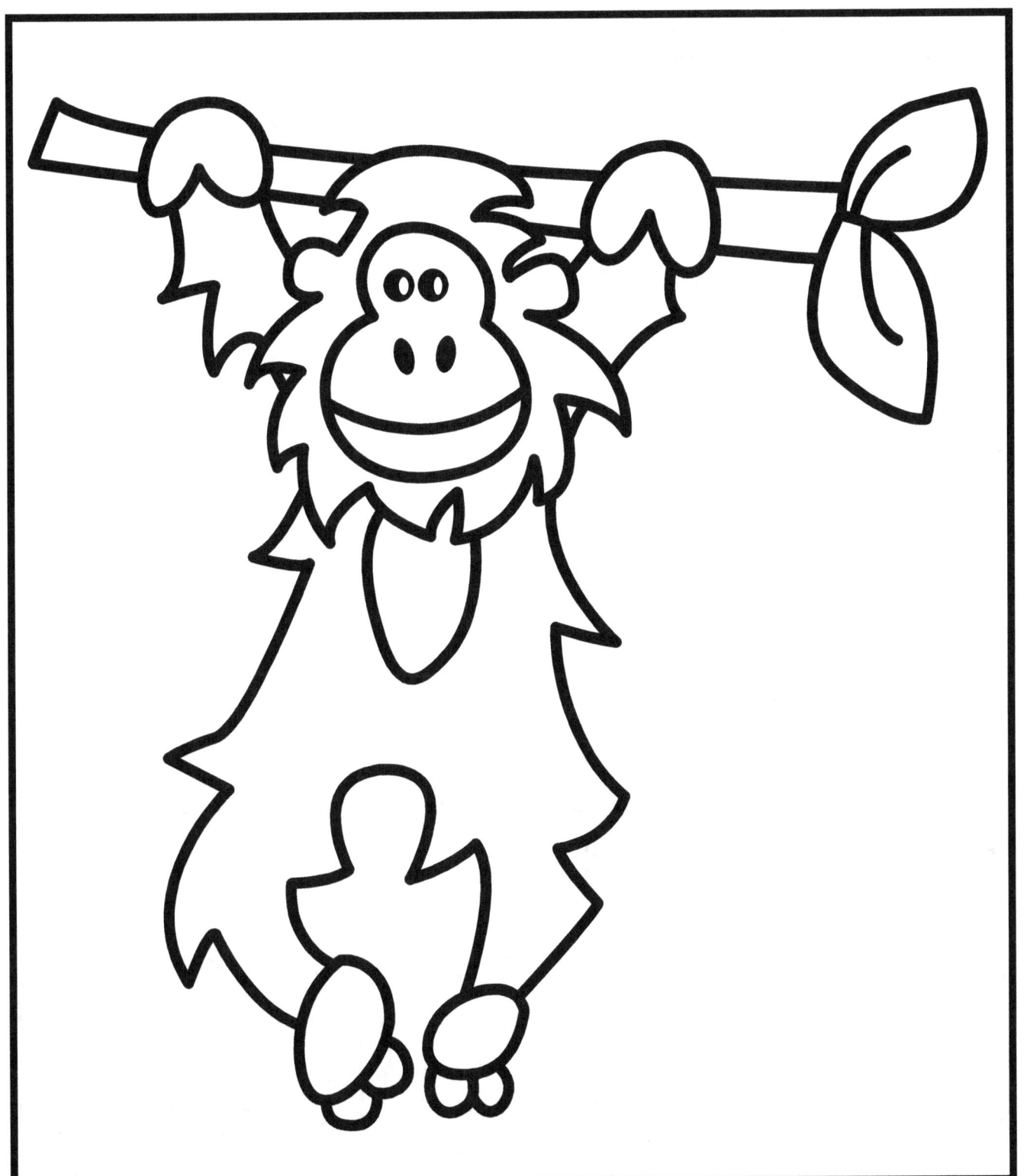

CONTRASTING COLORS

Contrast: A principle of design where light colors are used next to dark colors.

Test different color combinations on another piece of paper. Then copy the combinations that best match the descriptions below.

STRONGEST CONTRAST

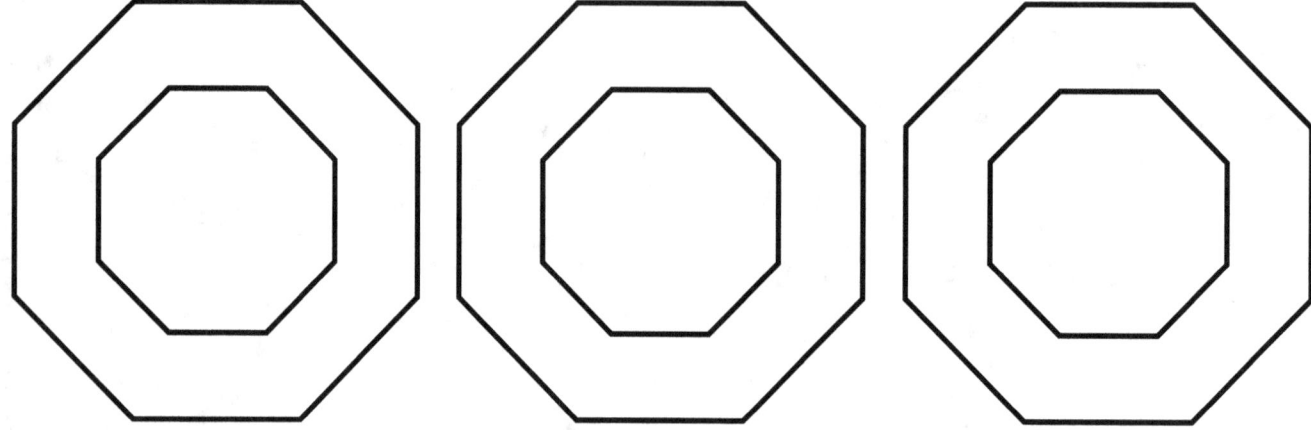

LEAST CONTRAST

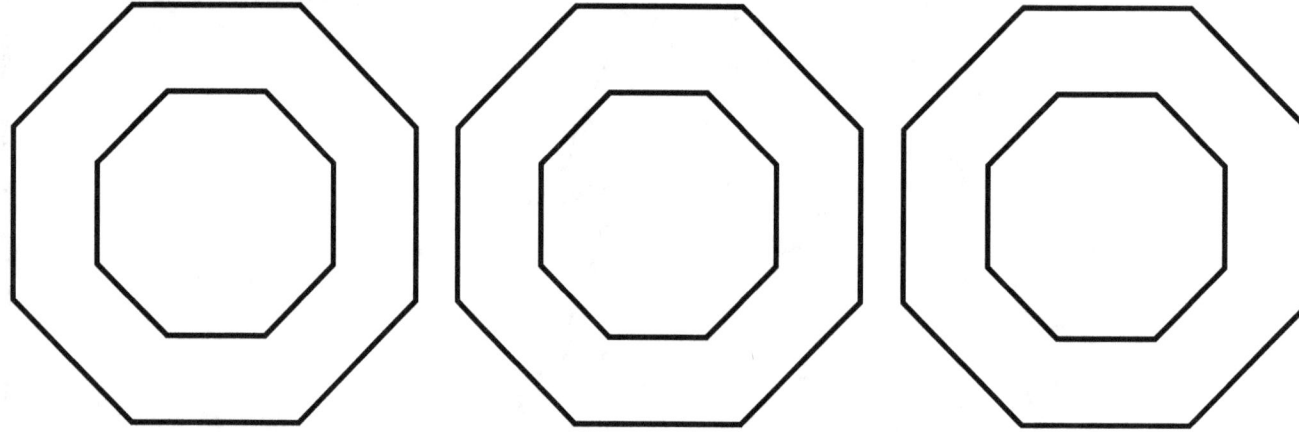

FAVORITE COMBINATIONS

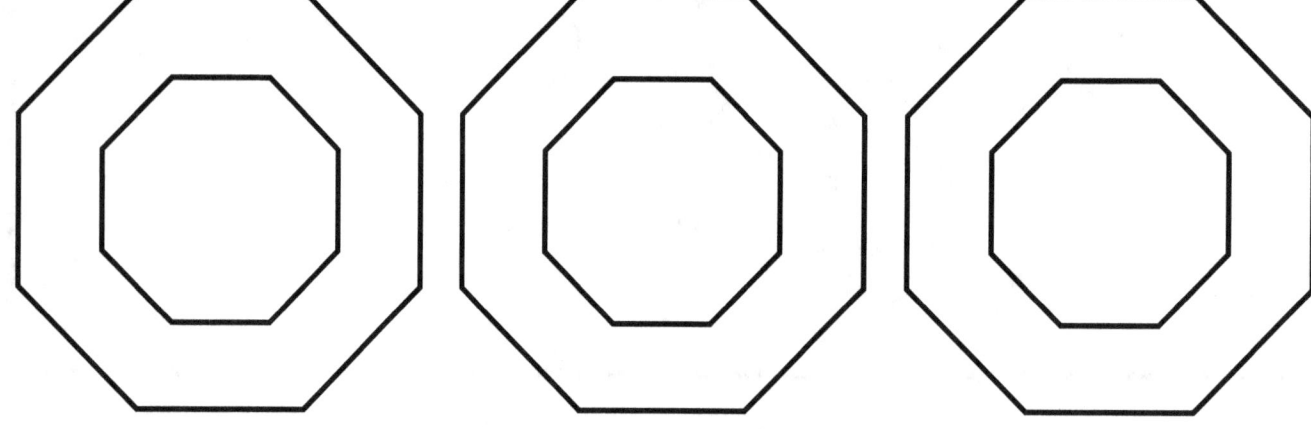

COMPLEMENTARY COLORS

Complementary colors: Colors opposite each other on the color wheel. For example: yellow and purple.

Color the picture using any 2 complementary colors.

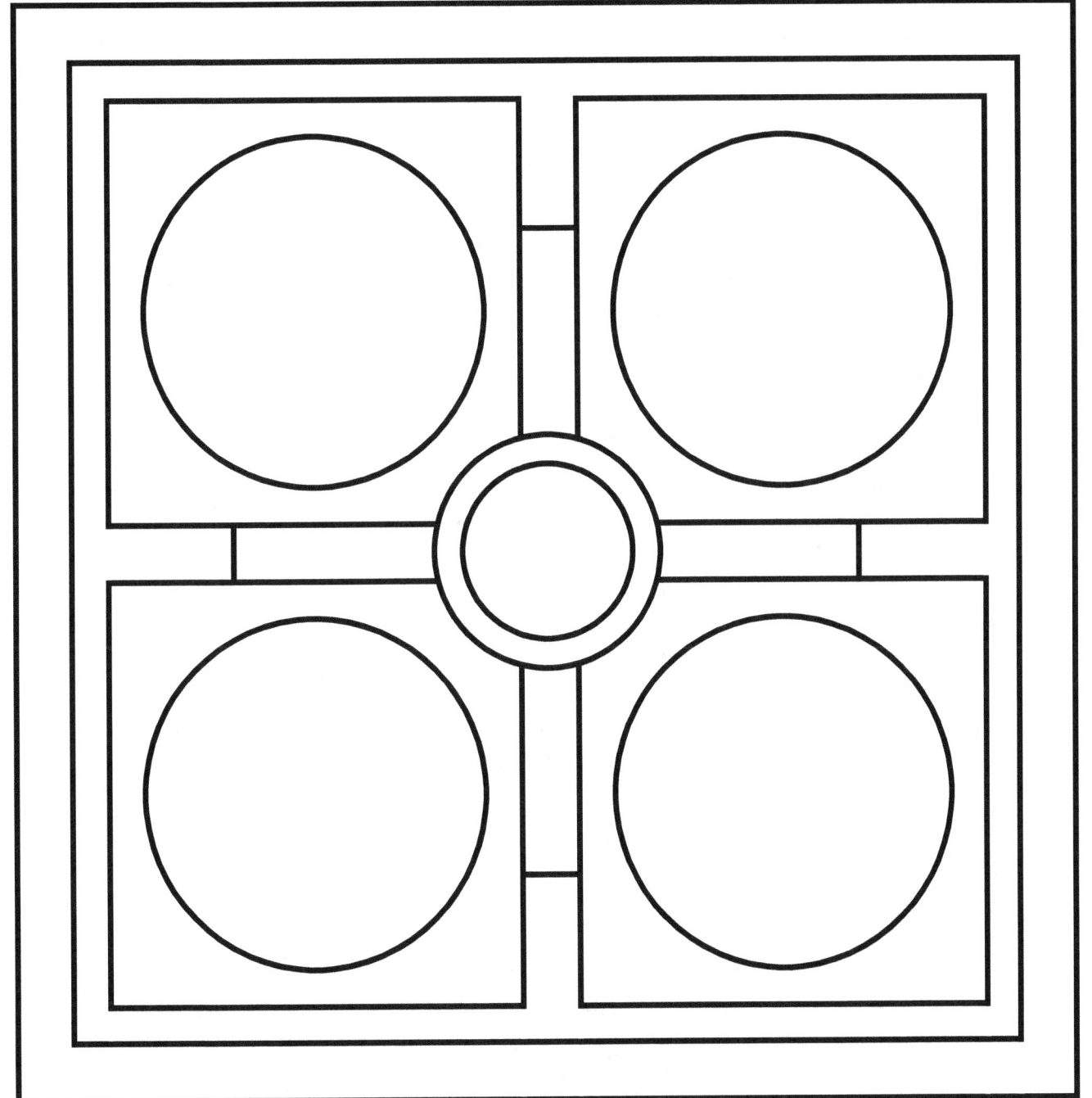

ELEMENTS OF DESIGN: VALUE

Shade: Dark value of a color made by adding black.

Using tempera paint, create shades of the following colors by adding black, a little bit at a time.

	Add one drop of black	**Add a little more...**	**Add a little more...**
RED			
GREEN			
ORANGE			
PURPLE			
BLUE			

ELEMENTS OF DESIGN: VALUE

Tint: Light value of a color made by adding white.

Using tempera paint, create tints of the following colors by adding white, a little bit at a time.

	Add one drop of white	**Add a little more...**	**Add a little more...**
RED			
GREEN			
ORANGE			
PURPLE			
BLUE			

MONOCHROMATIC FUN

Monochromatic: Made using different shades and tints of one color.

Color each rose in shades or tints of one color. Choose a different color for each rose. Make sure to fill in the background for each rose.

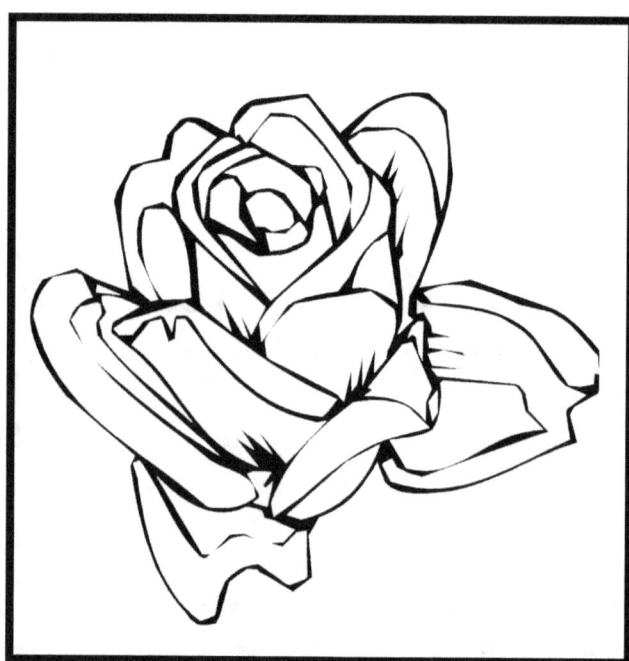
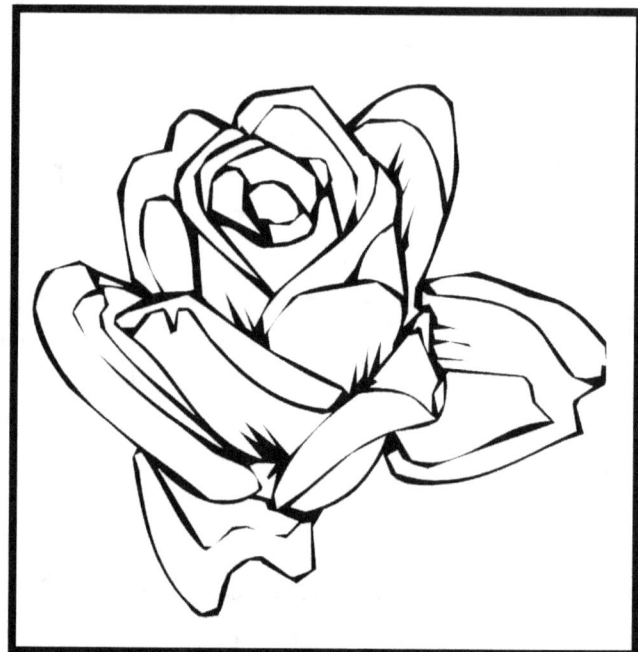
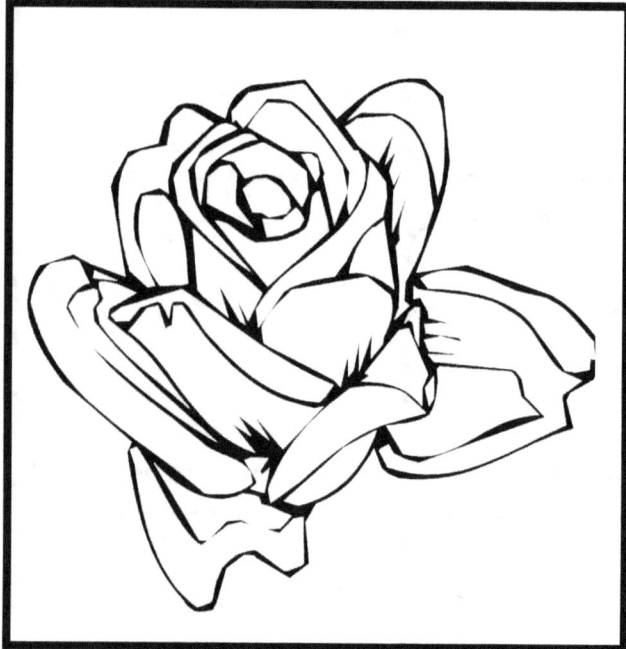
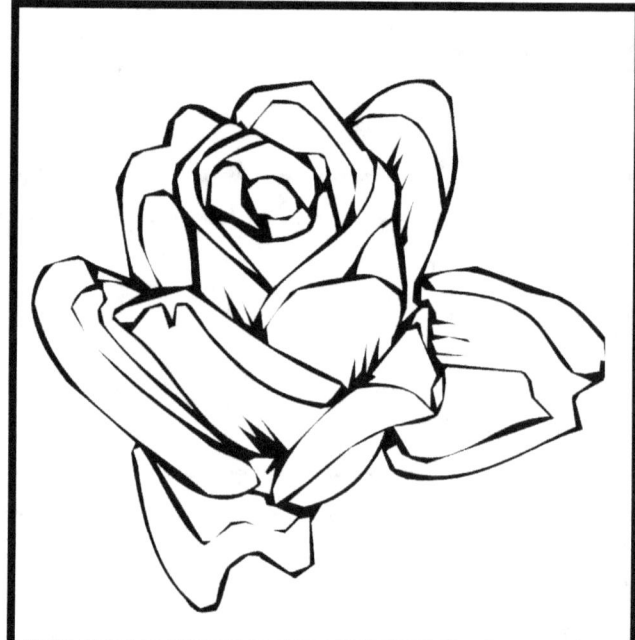

SHADES OF GRAY

Color the geometric design in different shades of gray.

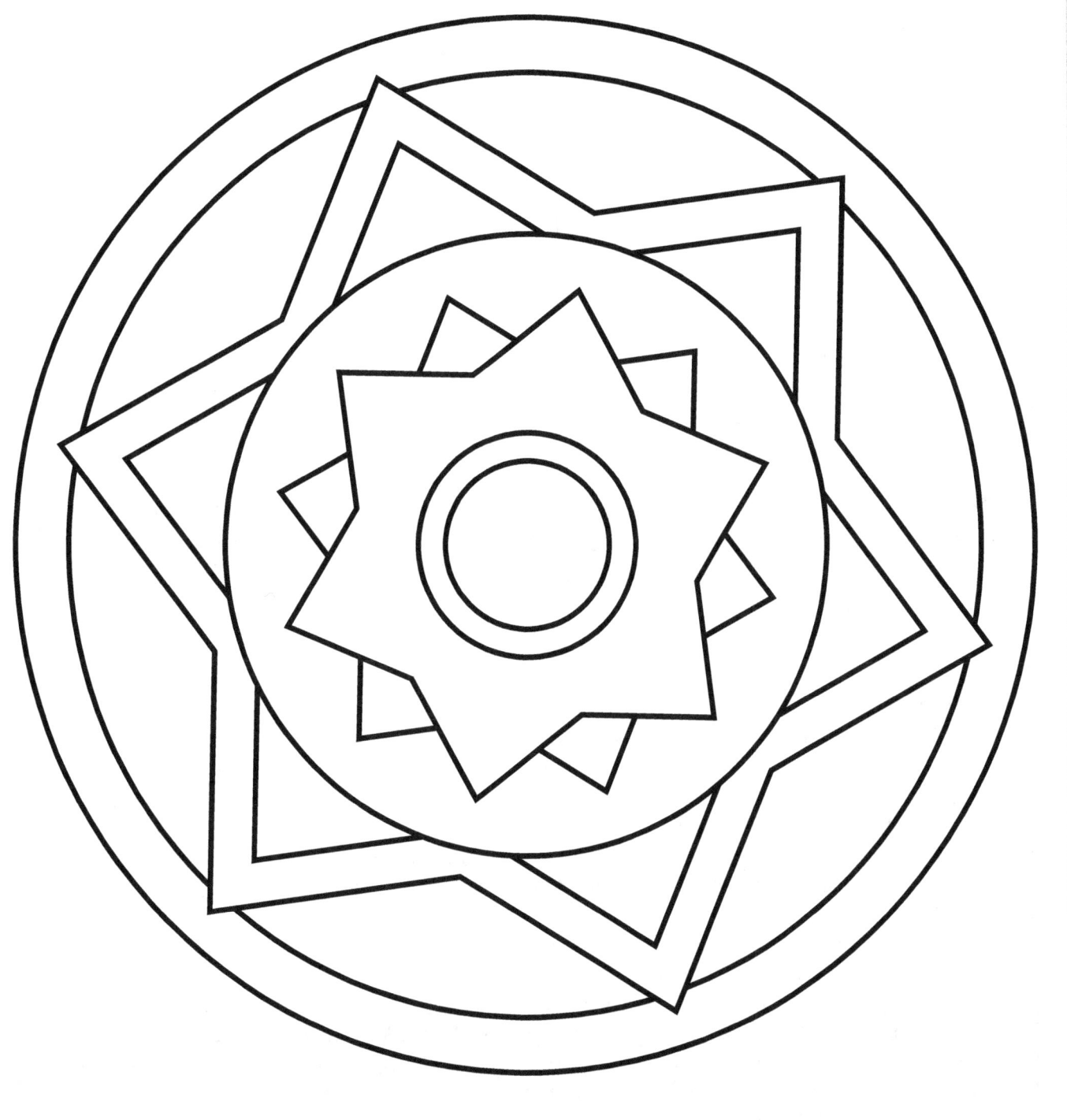

ELEMENTS OF DESIGN: LINE

Activity 1: Outlining Objects

What you need:

- Crayons
- Pastels
- Paint and paintbrushes
- A variety of everyday objects like scissors, drinking glasses, cans, or toothbrushes
- Paper
- Chalk
- Pencil crayons

What to do:

1. Demonstrate for students how to trace the contour of various objects to create a pleasing line composition.
2. Invite students to trace various objects and overlap them to create their own line compositions. Encourage students to use assorted drawing materials and colors and to notice the types of lines created by each.

Activity 2: Contour Drawing

What you need:

- Paper • Small fruits • HB pencil

What to do:

1. Explain to students that they will be completing a contour drawing of a small fruit such as a pear or banana. Review the term contour drawing.
2. Have students begin by placing the fruit of their choice near the paper. Students may find it helpful to strive to make their drawings the same size as the actual fruit.
3. Then encourage students to begin their contour drawing. They should choose a point on the edge of the fruit and follow its contour with their eyes, allowing their hand to copy the shape of the fruit onto the paper.
4. Caution students not to rush. They should try to draw every curve, including strong lines on the fruit such as a fold or crease.
5. Remind students that the purpose of this activity is to practice getting their hand and eye to do the same thing, by judging the size and shape of the edges the student can see.
6. Once done, have students review their drawings and consider whether their drawings match the real-life shapes of the fruit. Discuss whether the proportions are correct and whether enough details were included.
7. Repeat this drawing activity using different everyday objects.

ELEMENTS OF DESIGN: LINE

Activity 3: Rhythm and Line

What you need:
- Crayons
- Pastels
- Different types of music
- Paper
- Chalk
- Pencil crayons

What to do:

1. Choose and play a piece of music for students and have them trace the rhythm of the music with a finger in the air. Ask them to describe the line their finger creates.
2. Now have students draw the line that represents the rhythm of the music using the material(s) and color(s) of their choice. Have students add more such lines above and below the first line.
3. Repeat the activity with different types of music and discuss as a class why students chose the types of lines and colors they did.

Activity 4: Sgraffito

What you need:
- Paper (untextured)
- Crayons
- Paintbrushes
- Thick tempera paint
- Objects that scratch, such as, toothpicks, tongue depressors, combs, coins and plastic utensils

What to do:

1. Invite students to draw broad bands of color, using crayons, on a piece of paper that has a smooth surface. Remind students to apply pressure on the crayons as they draw.
2. Once completed, have students paint over the entire paper with the black tempera paint.
3. After the paint dries encourage students to scratch designs onto the paper using the objects. This technique is called sgraffito.

LINES, LINES, LINES!

Draw examples of the following lines.

Thin Lines
Thick Lines
Wavy Lines
Dotted Lines
Zigzag Lines
Horizontal Lines
Diagonal Lines
Vertical Lines

EXPLORING LINE

Using pencil crayons, fill in the sections of the picture by using different types of colored lines.

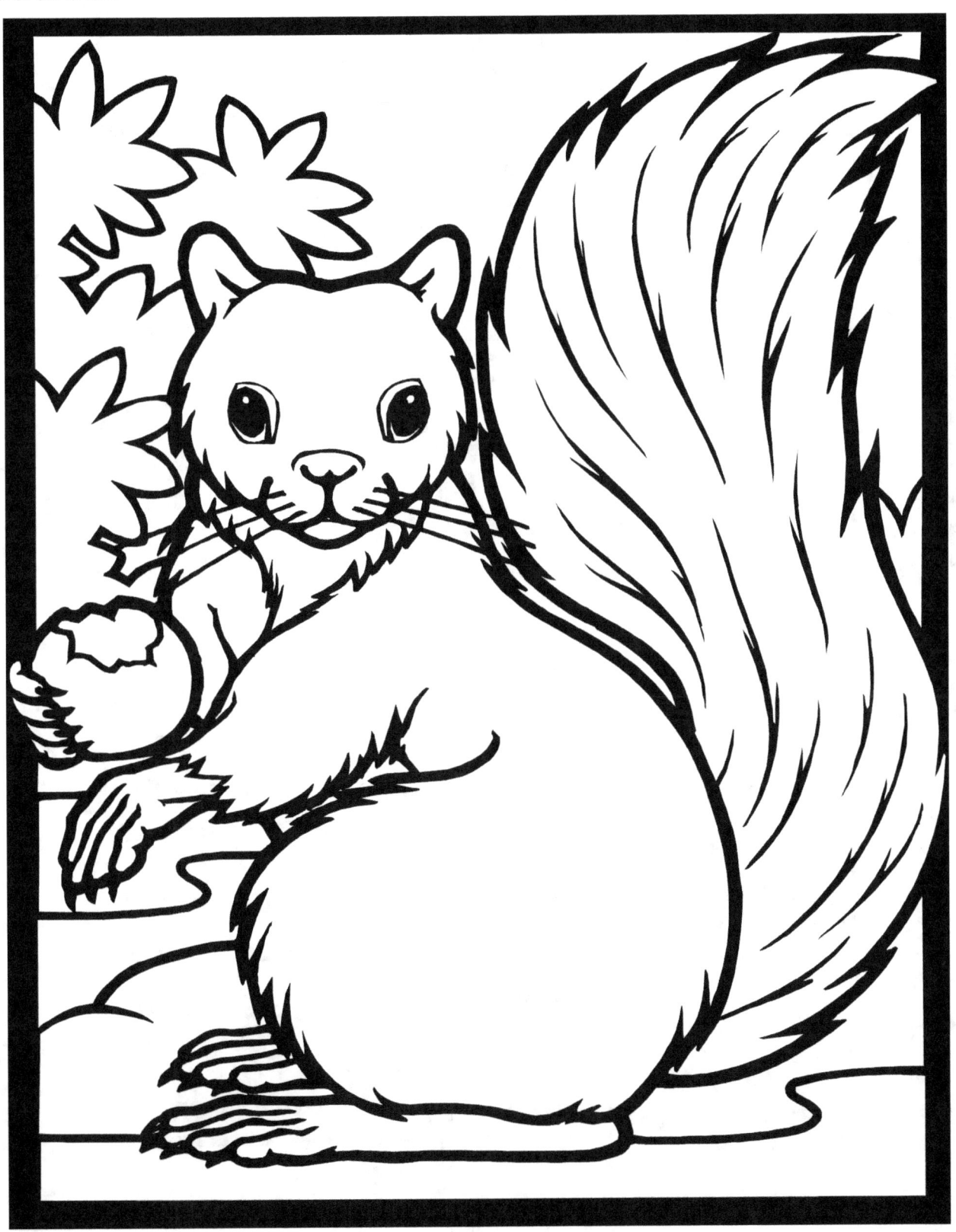

EXPLORING LINE

Using pencil crayons, fill in the sections of the picture by using different types of colored lines.

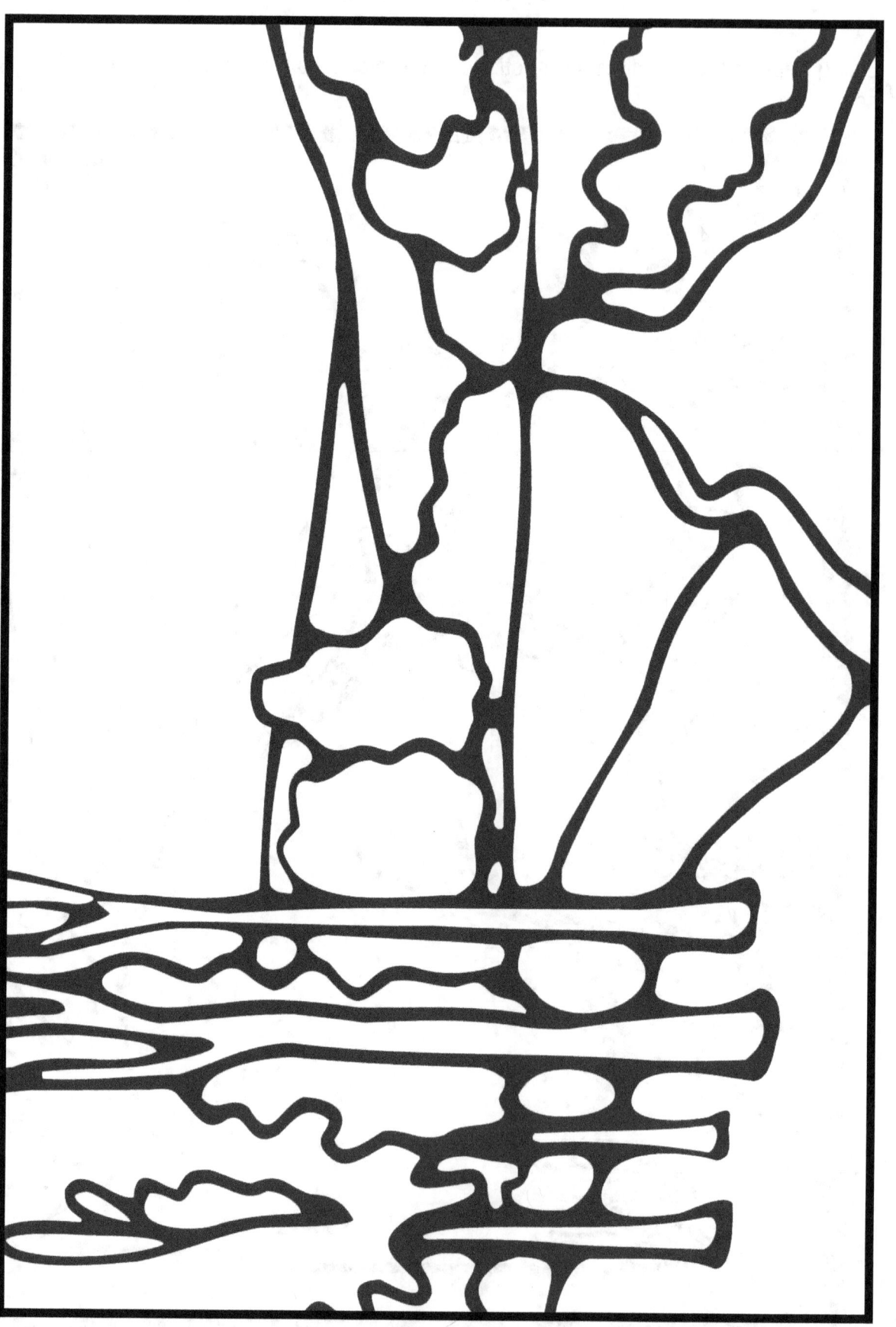

EXPLORING LINE

Fill in the sections of the picture by using different types of lines. Then, add a colorful patterned background.

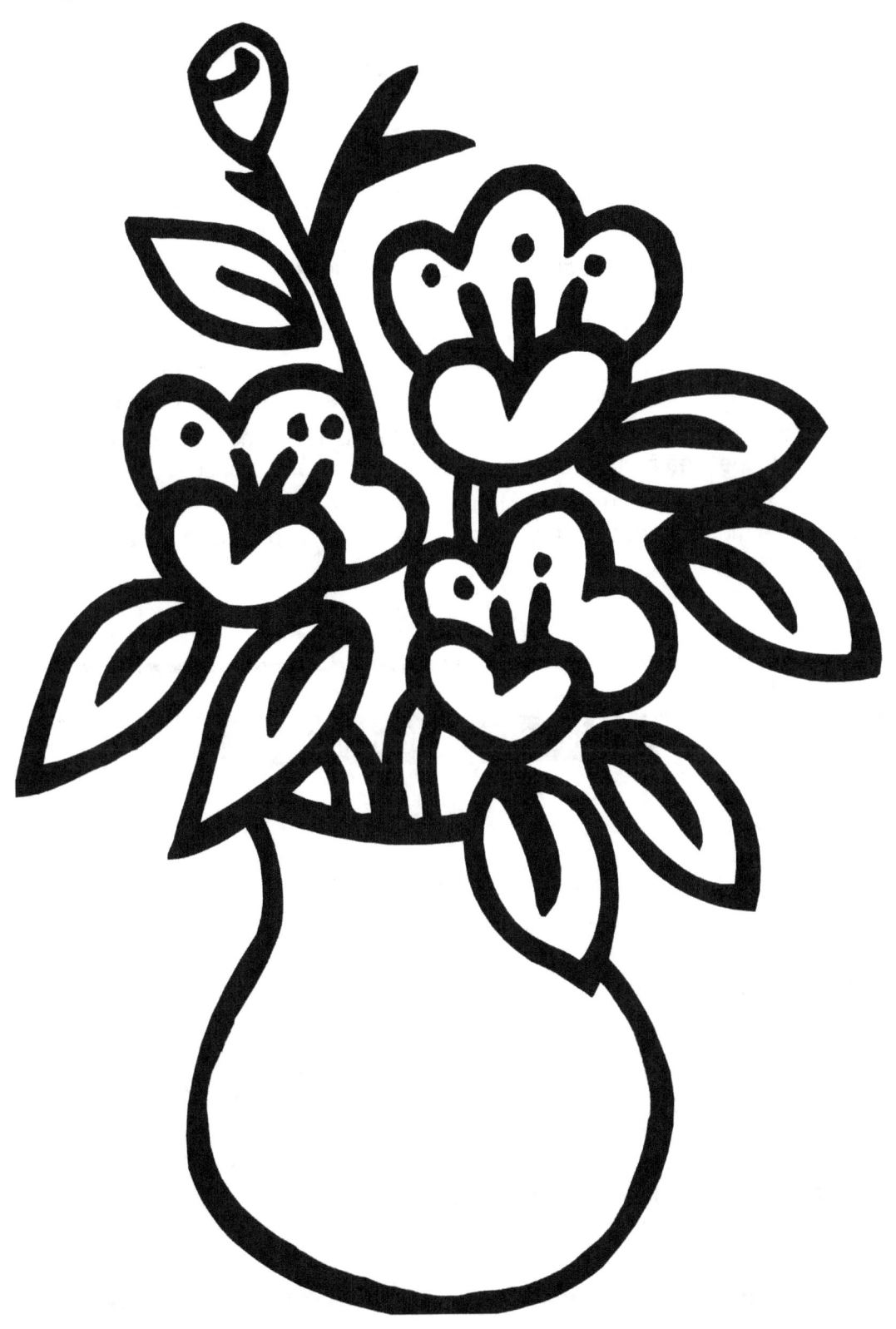

ELEMENTS OF DESIGN: FORM

Activity 1: Drawing People

What you need:

- White paper • Pencil and eraser • Coloring materials

What to do:

1. Demonstrate for students how the human body may be looked upon as a series of connected oval or sausage-like shapes.
2. Use a student as a model to draw, and help students see the breakdown of the oval body parts.
3. Once you have drawn all of the oval segments of the human form, erase the overlapping lines where body parts connect. Point out to students that there are joints where many body parts connect. Joints include the shoulders, knees and wrists.
4. Next, add clothing and other features to complete the drawing. Show students how to add lines to the area around joints to show bent limbs and creases.
5. Students are now ready to draw their humans. Have students work in pairs, so that they can be models for each other. Encourage students to draw their partners in various positions.

Activity 2: Animated People

What you need:

- White paper • Pencil and eraser • Coloring materials

What to do:

1. Review with students how the human body may be looked upon as a series of connected oval or sausage-like shapes.
2. Next, have students work in pairs. One partner will pose while the other partner will draw the partner in a series of 3–5 positions that show action, such as when participating in a sport.
3. Encourage students to draw details on their animated person and facial expressions.
4. Students should also add a background to their picture.

SCULPTURE FUN

Give students opportunities to sculpt and paint different forms. In addition to dough (see recipes below), provide students with cookie cutters, rollers, plastic knives, plastic spoons, and wooden craft sticks as well as paints and paintbrushes. Demonstrate for students how to roll, flatten, and pinch dough to form shapes. You may also provide students with wiggle eyes, buttons, and pipe cleaners to add to their sculptures. Store dough in sealed containers.

Self-Hardening Dough

- 1 1/2 cups water
- 1 1/2 cups salt
- 4 cups flour
- 1 teaspoon alum

1. Mix dry ingredients in a bowl.
2. Gradually add water.
3. Knead until the mixture is pliable.

Sand Sculpture Dough

- 4 cups clean sand (not beach sand)
- 2 cups cornstarch
- 2 cups water

1. Mix all ingredients in a saucepan.
2. Heat the mixture over medium heat and stir until it becomes as thick as modeling clay.
3. Once the mixture is the right consistency, allow it to cool before handling.

Smelly Modeling Dough

- 3 cups flour
- 1/2 cup salt
- 2 packages flavored drink crystals
- 2 cups boiling water

1. Mix dry ingredients in a bowl.
2. Add boiling water.
3. Mix and knead on a floured surface.

LINES OF SYMMETRY

Draw the other half of the picture. Color the picture.

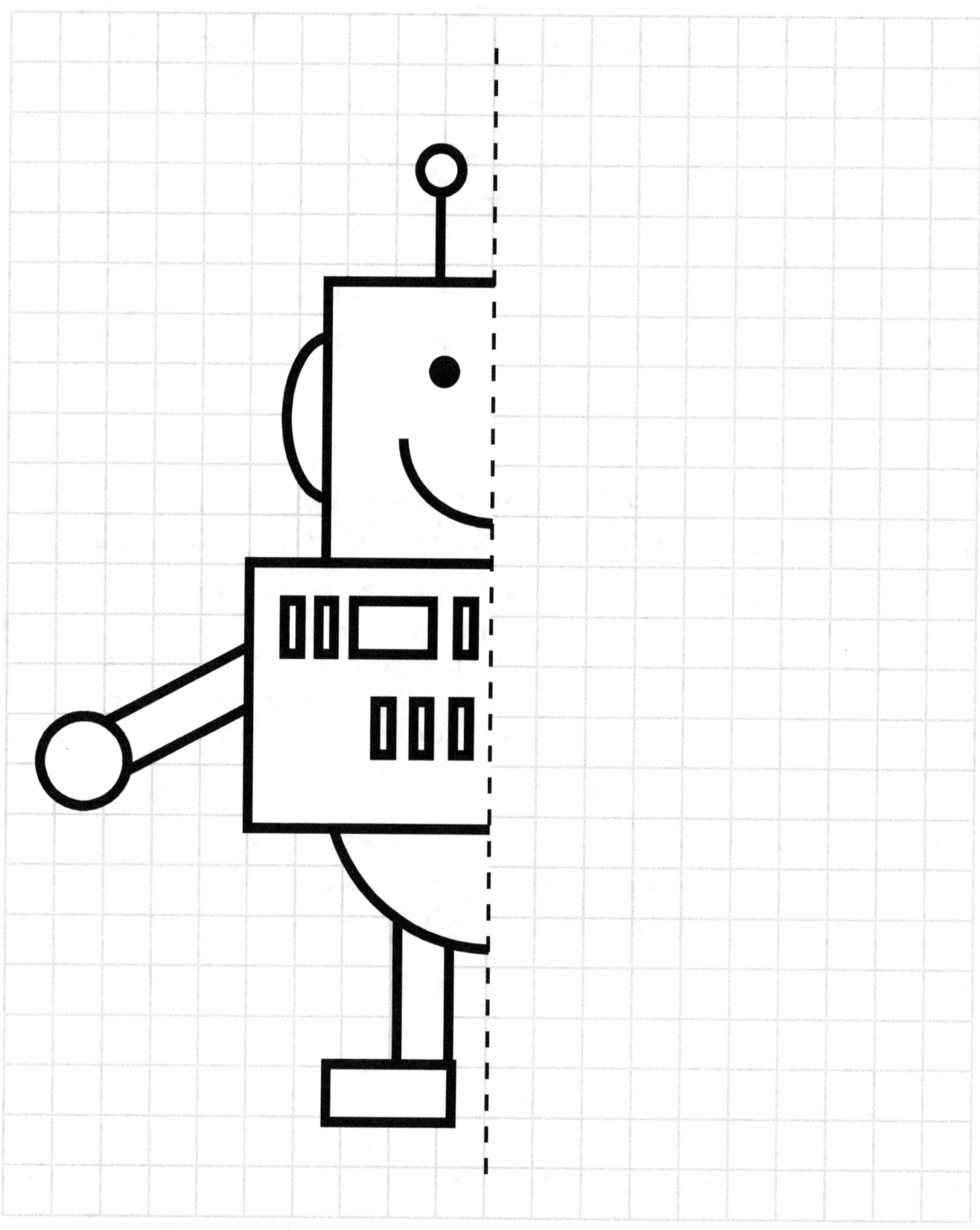

ORIGAMI DOLL

What you need:
- A square piece of white paper
- Coloring materials

What to do:

1.
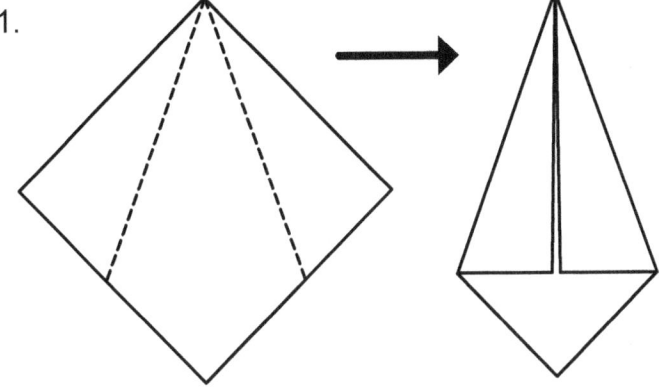
Demonstrate for students how to fold two edges of the square to the center line to form a diamond shape.

2.
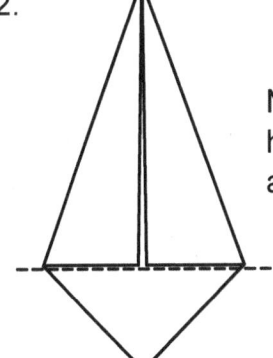
Next, show students how to fold the triangle at the bottom up.

3.
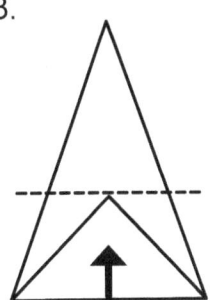
Now, make a fold near the center of the triangle, bringing the bottom part up over the top part.

4.
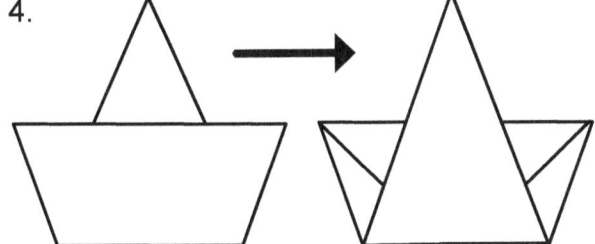
Then, demonstrate how to flip the entire origami piece over.

5.
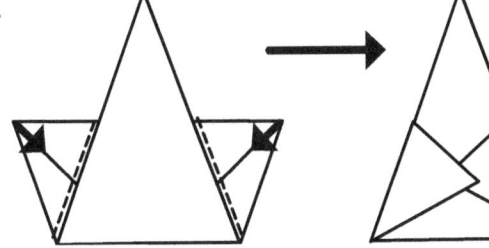
Lastly, show students how to fold each of the two triangular flaps toward the center. These will be the doll's arms.

6.
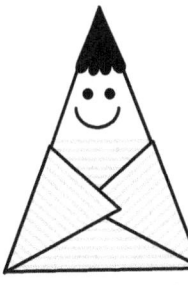
Encourage students to draw and color a face, hair, clothes, hands, and other details.

FANTASY CREATURE FILL-IN

Use these body parts to draw your own fantasy creature.

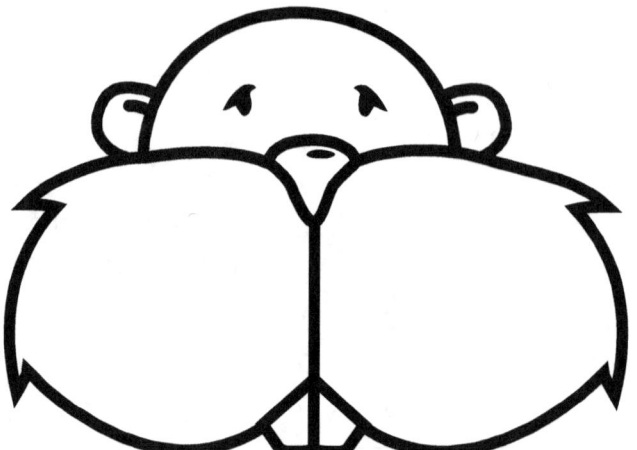
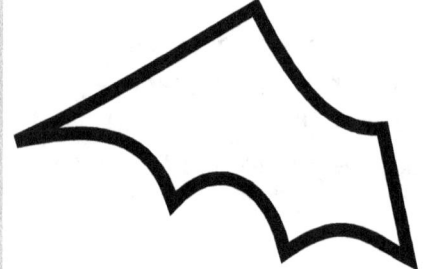
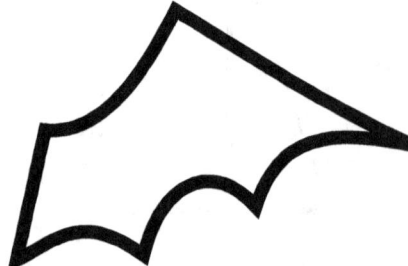

BRAIN STRETCH: On a separate piece of paper, create your own fantasy creature.

ELEMENTS OF DESIGN: TEXTURE

Activity 1: Fruit and Veggie Printmaking

What you need:

- Cut sections of a variety of fruit and vegetables
- Styrofoam plates
- Tempera paint in assorted colors
- Paper

What to do:

1. Pour tempera paint onto Styrofoam plates, one color per plate.
2. Demonstrate for students how to carefully press cut sections of vegetables or fruit into the paint and then press those paint-laden sections onto paper to create a print. Remind students not to drag the fruit or vegetable across the page.
3. Encourage students to create patterns or designs with one or more sections of fruit or vegetable.
4. Invite students to share and discuss their prints with each other. How did they create different patterns? Which fruits or vegetables produced the best prints?

Activity 2: Monoprints

What you need:

- Printmaking ink or tempera paint with flour added to make its consistency thicker
- Paintbrushes
- Small sheets of Plexiglass
- Paper
- A covered work area

What to do:

1. Tell students that monoprints are unique: only one print is made from the printing plate.
2. Demonstrate for students how to paint a design or picture onto the Plexiglass. Emphasize that students must work quickly so that the paint won't dry.
3. Next, show students how to place the paper over the Plexiglass and press lightly with the palm of the hand, to transfer the design onto the paper.
4. Peel away the paper and admire the monoprint!

EXPERIMENT WITH TEXTURE

Encourage students to create different textures with the tools, materials, and papers listed below. They can use the textures to create a collage or to fill sections of a picture.

Out-of-the-Ordinary Painting Tools

- Fingers
- Sticks
- Blocks of wood
- Branches
- Rope
- Feathers
- Leaves
- Sponges
- Tissues
- Brushes
- Cotton swabs
- Cotton balls
- Plastic pot scrubbers
- Plastic wrap
- Makeup brushes

Excellent Drawing and Painting Materials

- Crayons
- Pencils
- Pastels
- Chalk
- Charcoal
- Ink pen
- Water-based markers
- Acrylic paint
- Makeup
- Tempera paint
- Felt tip pens
- Pencil crayons
- Watercolors
- Food coloring

A Variety of Surfaces on Which to Paint or Draw

- Newsprint
- Paper plates
- Blocks of wood
- Tissue paper
- Paper bags
- Sandpaper
- Wet paper
- Cardboard
- Fabric
- Plastic wrap
- Paper towels
- Waxed paper
- Aluminum foil
- Stones
- Foam

CREATE DIFFERENT TEXTURES

Corn Syrup Paint

Make a striking paint with an interesting texture by combining food coloring and light corn syrup. Mix up as many colors as needed. Encourage students to paint different landscapes or oceanscapes. Students may wish to first create an outline drawing with a permanent marker before painting. Be sure to allow more than a day of drying time.

Flour-and-Water Finger Paint

This paint will help you to achieve great textures when finger painting. Mix 1 cup flour, 1 cup water and 2 teaspoons salt in a small container to make a paint with the consistency of thick gravy. Add in the desired food coloring. Repeat the process for as many colors as needed.

Glossy Paint

Give tempera paint a wet, glossy look by combining 1 part white glue and 1 part tempera paint.

Puff Paint

Have students create unique pictures using puff paint. Combine 1 cup salt, 1 cup sugar and the desired food coloring in a squeeze bottle. Shake the ingredients and squeeze the paint out of the bottle onto the paper.

Sand Paint

Sand paint offers an interesting option when striving to create texture in a picture. Begin by having students create a simple outline drawing. Then make the sand paint by combining 1 part sand and 5 parts powdered tempera. Encourage students to experiment when mixing the sand and tempera to achieve the desired color. Next, when a few sand paint colors have been made, use a wooden craft stick to spread a thin layer of glue in one section of the outline drawing. Then, using a spoon, gently pour the sand paint into the glue-covered section. Lightly lift the paper to shake off any excess sand paint. Allow the sand painting to dry, and seal it using hair spray.

Wax Resist

As wax and water don't mix, the wax resist technique can be used to mask out areas to preserve the white of the paper or the color beneath and to create appealing textures. Draw or color with a wax crayon and then wash over it with a water-based paint.

EXPLORING TEXTURE

Pointillism: A technique of painting in which tiny dots of color are placed close together. From a distance, the dots seem to disappear and the colors blend.

Fill in sections of the landscape using only small dots of color. Use markers.

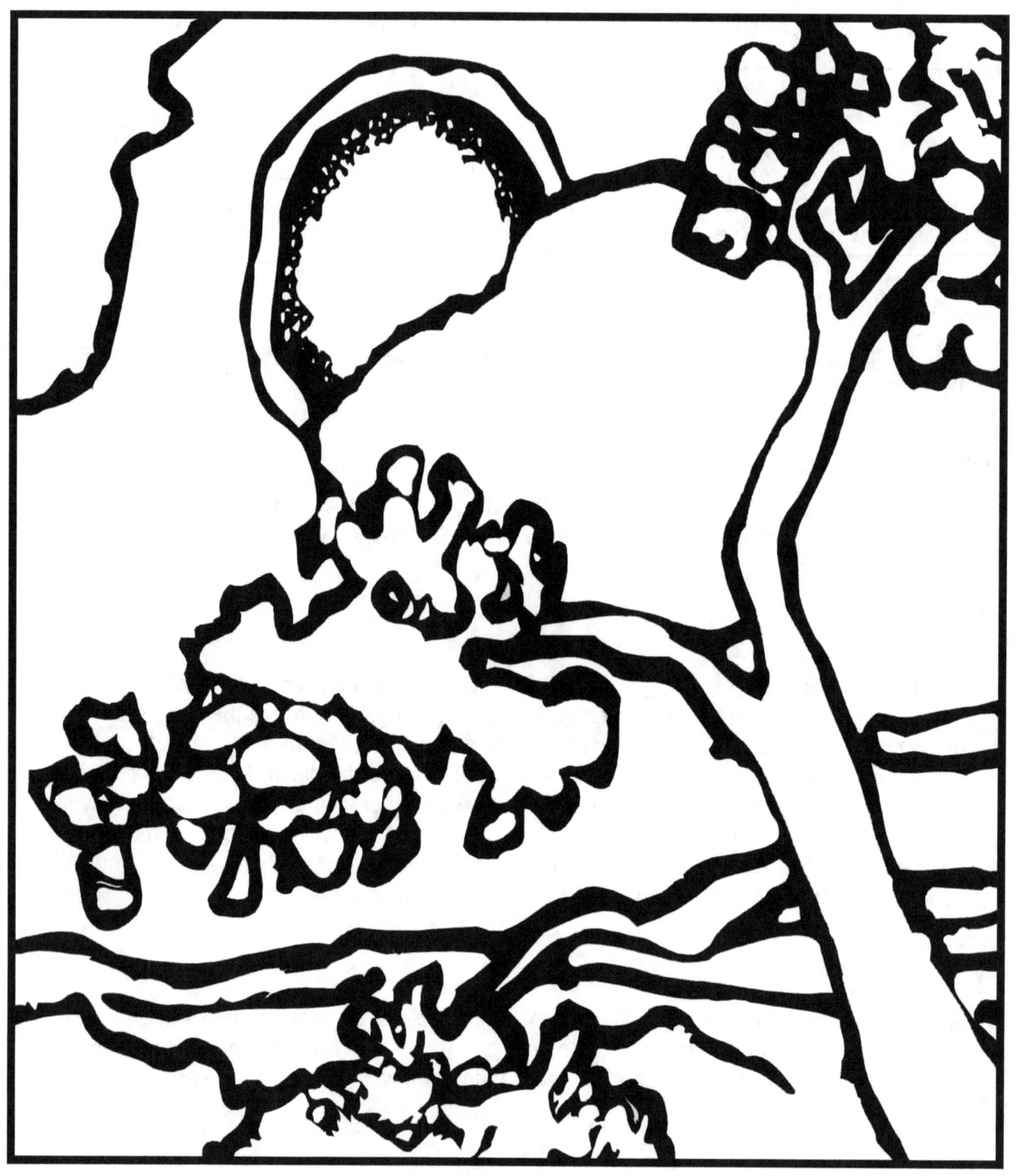

EXPLORING TEXTURE

Fill in sections of the picture by pasting torn bits of colored construction paper.

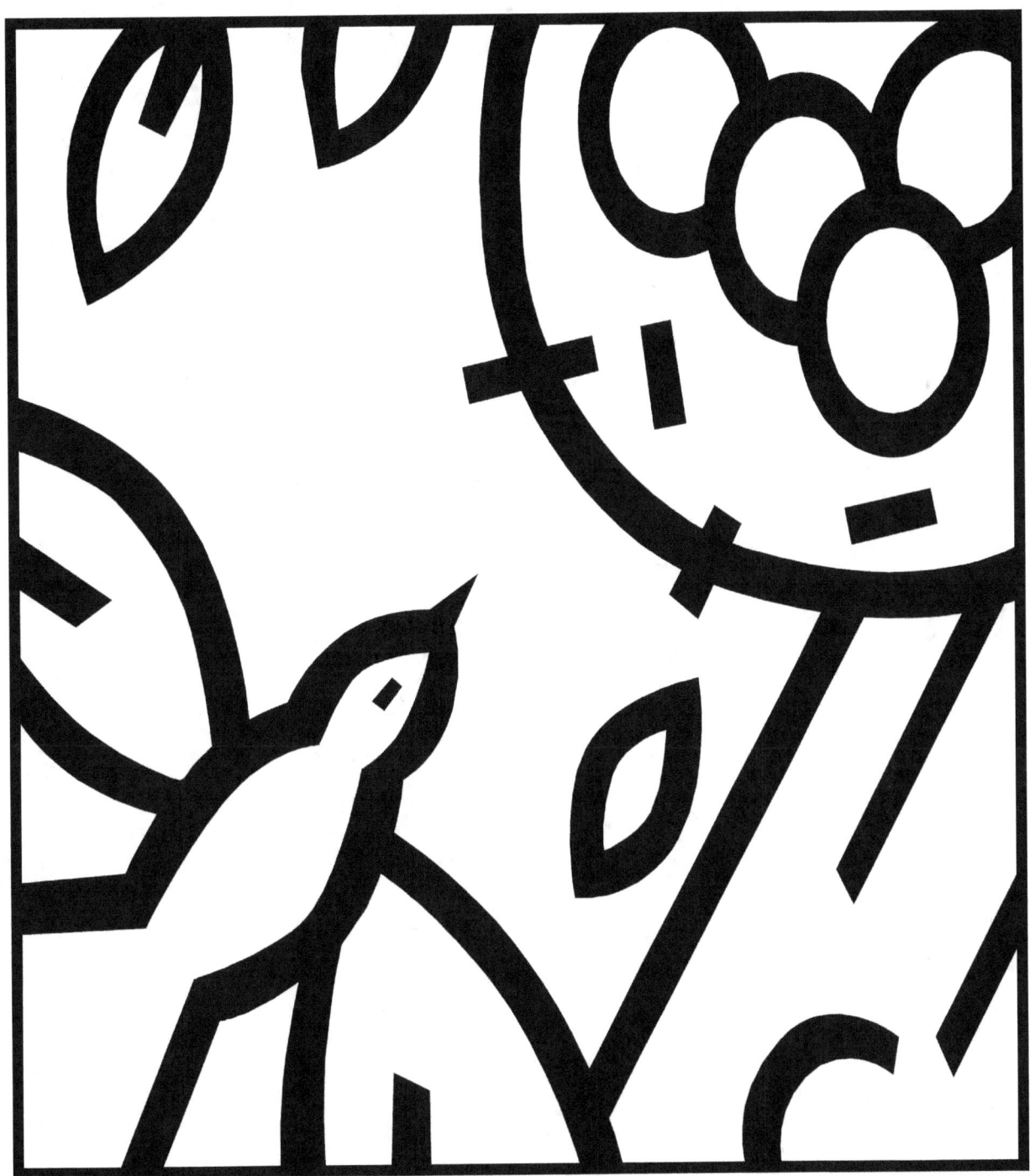

BRAIN STRETCH: Draw the outline of a new picture with a black marker and fill it in the same way.

EXPLORING TEXTURE

Paint the landscape at sunset using watercolors.

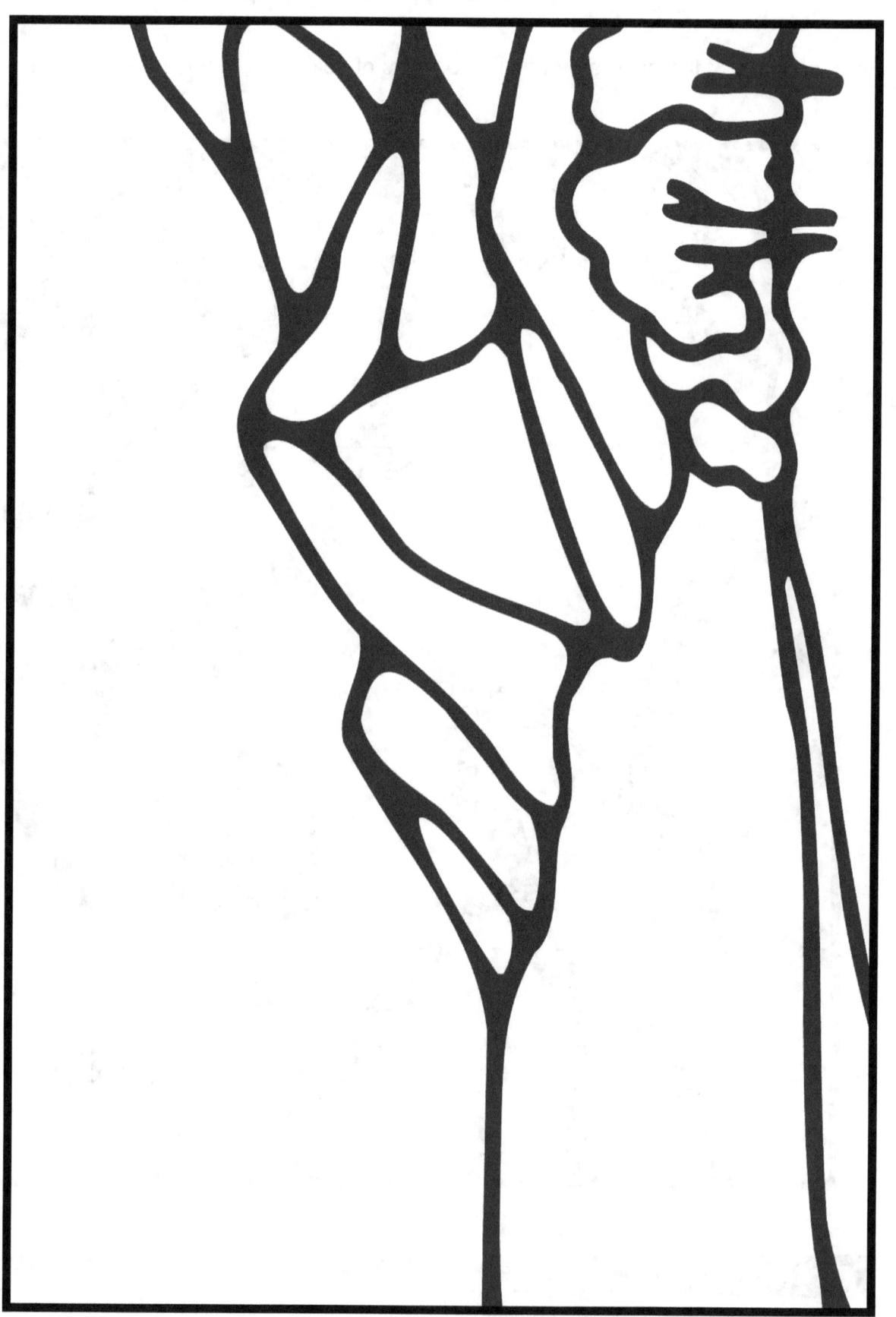

EXPLORING TEXTURE

Color the landscape using oil pastels and set it with hair spray.

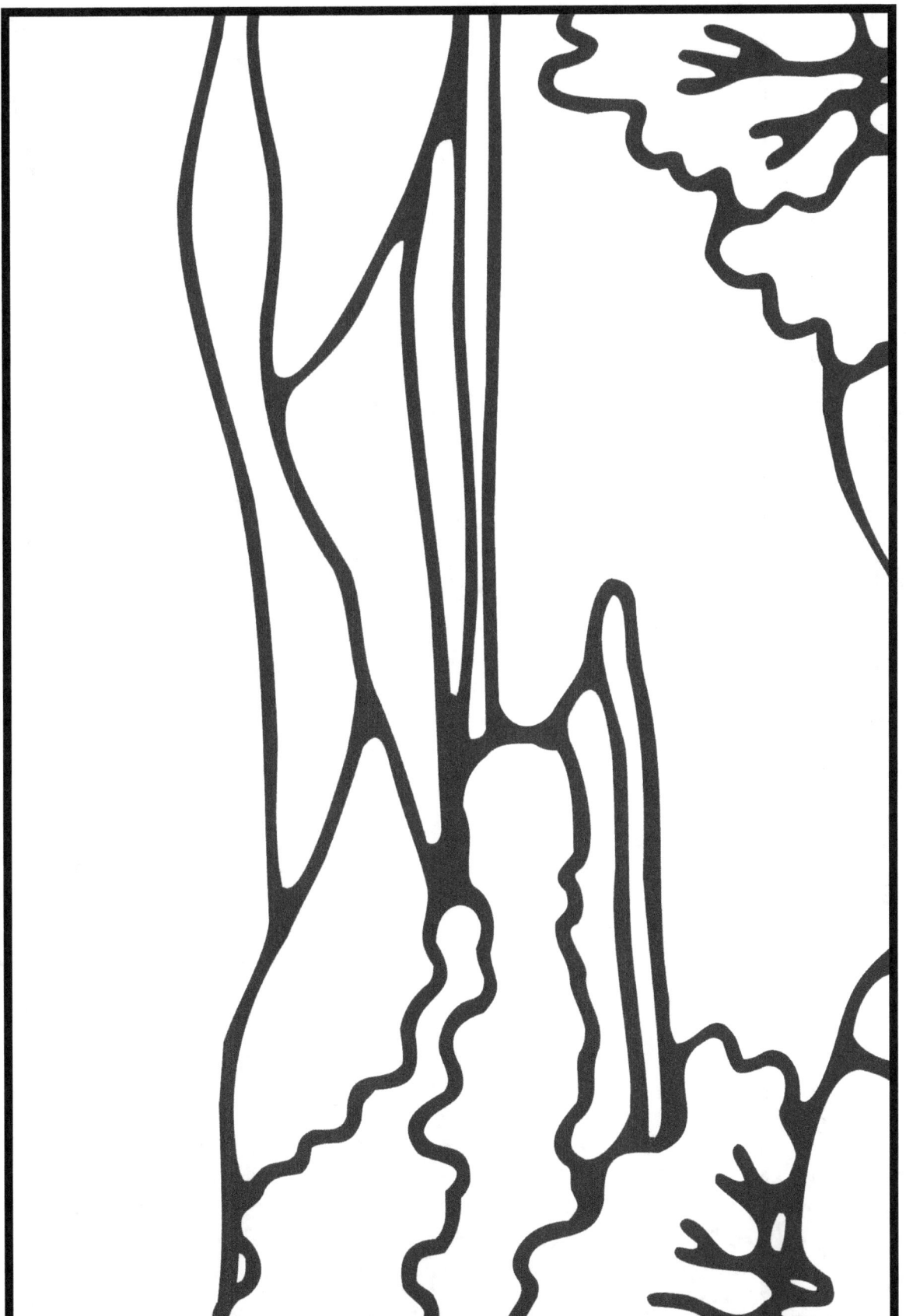

EXPLORING TEXTURE

Fill in sections of the landscape using different colors of Plasticine. Paint the sky using sunset colors.

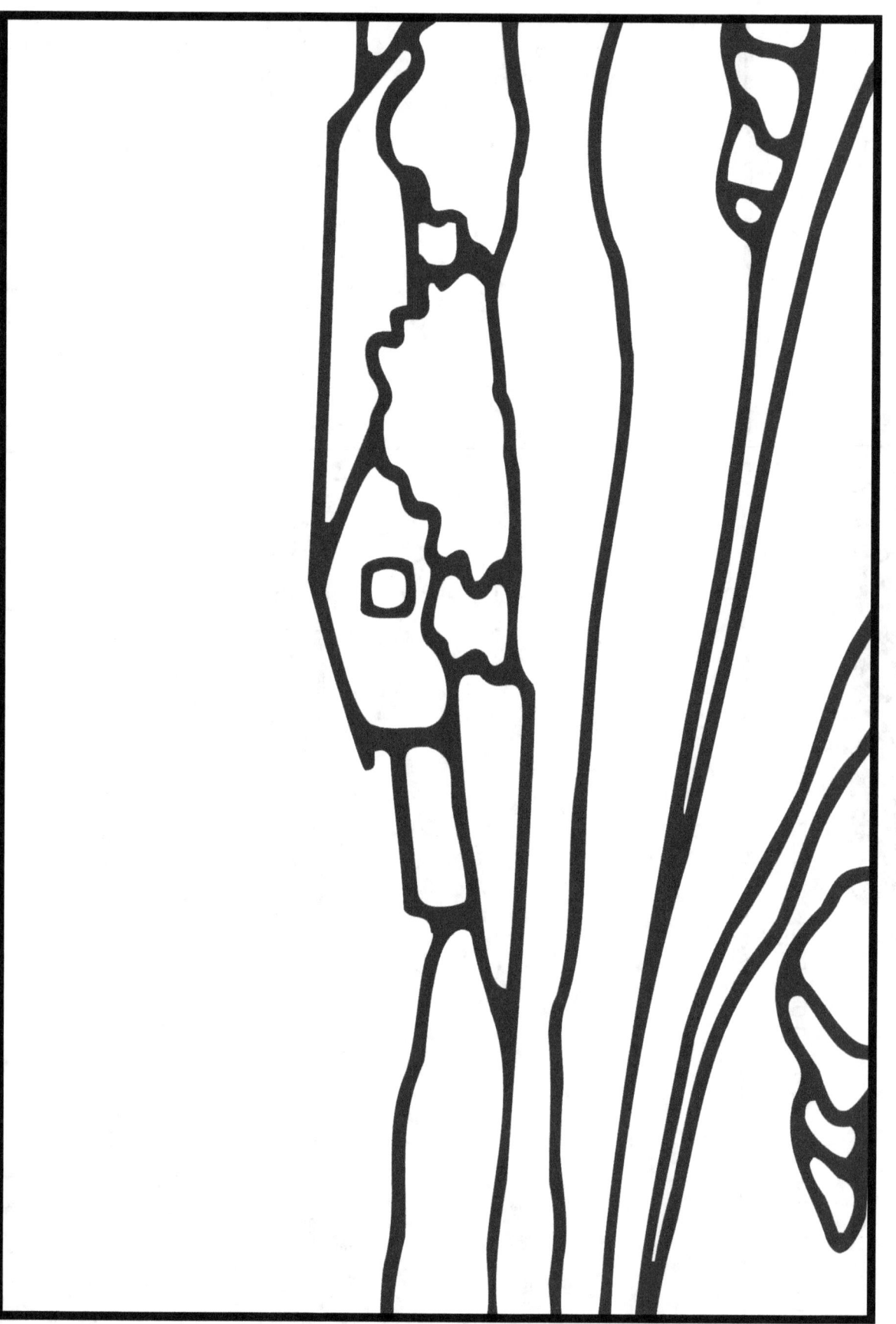

© Chalkboard Publishing

EXPLORING TEXTURE

Fill in sections of the picture using different textures.

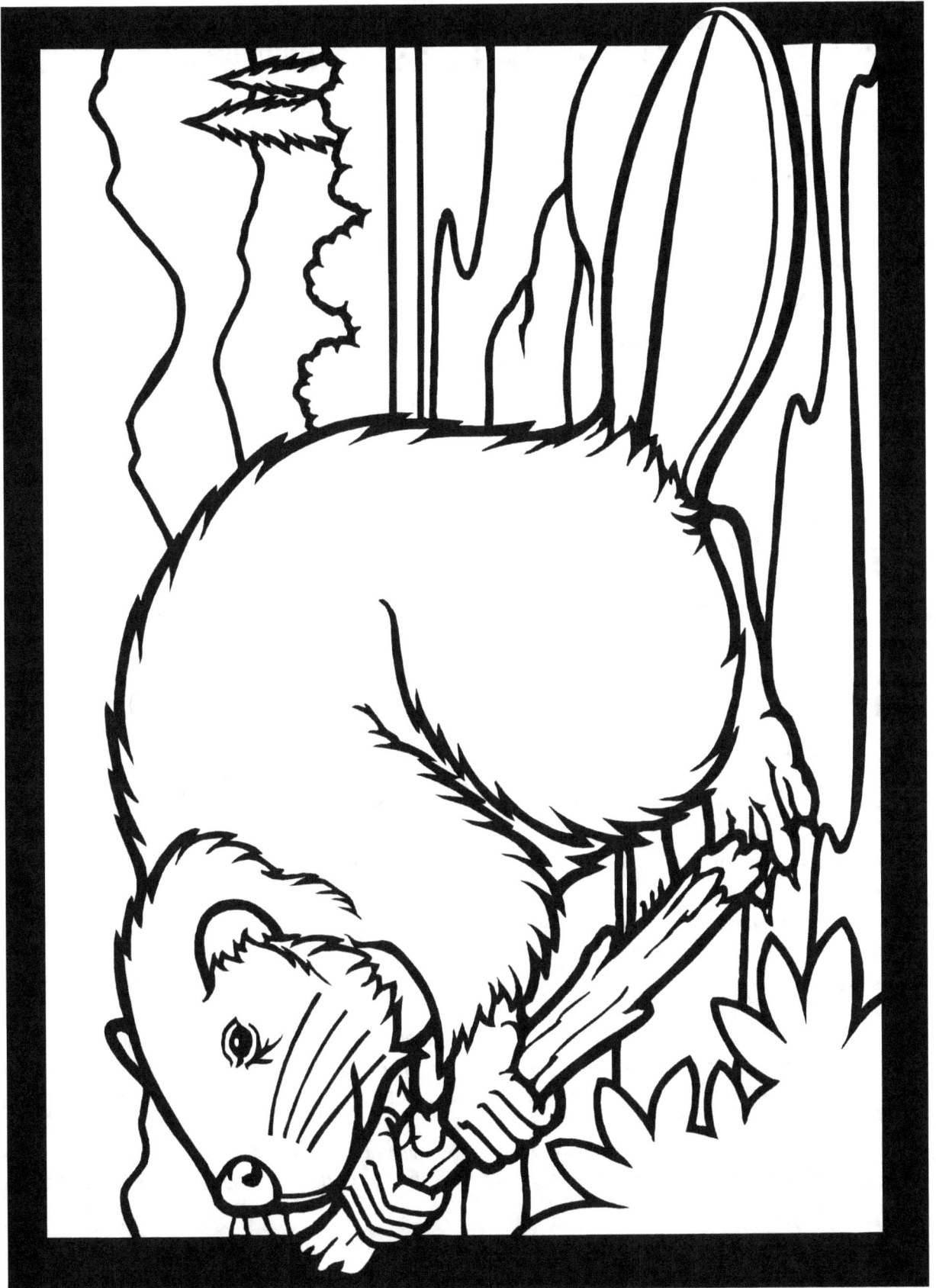

31

© Chalkboard Publishing

ELEMENTS OF DESIGN: SPACE

Activity 1: Focal Point of a Composition

What you need:

- Coloring materials, such as oil pastels, pencil crayons, or crayons
- Large sheets of paper
- Students' favorite stuffed animals or toys

What to do:

1. Discuss with students the concept of a focal point in a composition. The focal point draws a viewer's eye first. Explain how objects that are smaller than the focal point appear to be farther away from the viewer.
2. Instruct students to begin a composition by drawing their stuffed animal or toy and making it the focal point. Tell students that their stuffed animal should be as tall as a ruler.
3. Next, have students add a background to their composition. They should add a horizon line and objects that are farther away (and so smaller). Students can brainstorm possible locations for the stuffed animal (e.g., bedroom, forest) and think about the details of the location they choose.
4. Have students color their completed composition. Encourage students not to leave any blank areas.

Activity 2: Fill In the Missing Pieces

What you need:

- A picture cut from a magazine or calendar (e.g., car, flower, nature scene)
- Thick, white paper the same size as the magazine or calendar cutout
- Scissors
- Glue
- Crayons, colored pencils or oil pastels

What to do:

1. First, demonstrate for students how to cut their picture into wide diagonal strips.
2. Next, show students how to glue half of the picture strips onto the white paper, positioning every other piece where it would be if the picture were in one piece but leaving lots of space between the strips.
3. Then, have students draw and color in the missing sections of the picture, using the media of their choice. Students can use their imagination or common sense to fill in the missing sections.

ELEMENTS OF DESIGN: SPACE

Activity 3: Landscape

What you need:
- White paper
- Oil pastels
- Cotton balls for smudging

What to do:

1. Review with students the art terms foreground, middle ground and background and tell them that they will be painting a landscape. Look at and discuss examples of landscapes.

2. To begin, show students how to lightly sketch with their pencil these three sections using ground, water and ground.

3. Instruct students to fill each section with paint. Encourage students to mix colors and to use more than one shade or tint of color.

4. Once the sections are completely covered with paint, have students add details and objects to the sections using darker colors. Remind students that objects in the foreground are the most prominent and appear to be the closest to the viewer. Alternatively, objects that are smaller are intended to appear farther away from the viewer.

Activity 4: Streetscape in One-Point Perspective

What you need:
- Coloring materials
- Pencil
- Eraser
- Ruler

What to do:

1. Review with students the art terms perspective, horizon line and vanishing point. Show examples of each term and how they are used in artwork.

2. Explain to students that they will draw a streetscape in one-point perspective. Have students begin by drawing a horizon line on their papers.

3. Next, students should find the midpoint of the horizon line and mark it as the vanishing point for their drawing.

4. Demonstrate for students how to mark the bottom right and left corners of their paper and then draw a line from each mark to the vanishing point. This will create the illusion of a street.

5. Have students add three-dimensional buildings along each side of the street. Remind students that buildings should decrease in size as they approach the vanishing point.

6. Encourage students to add other details to their drawings, both along the street and along the horizon line.

EXPLORING SPACE

Complete the picture by adding a horizon line and vanishing point. Add details to the picture and color it.

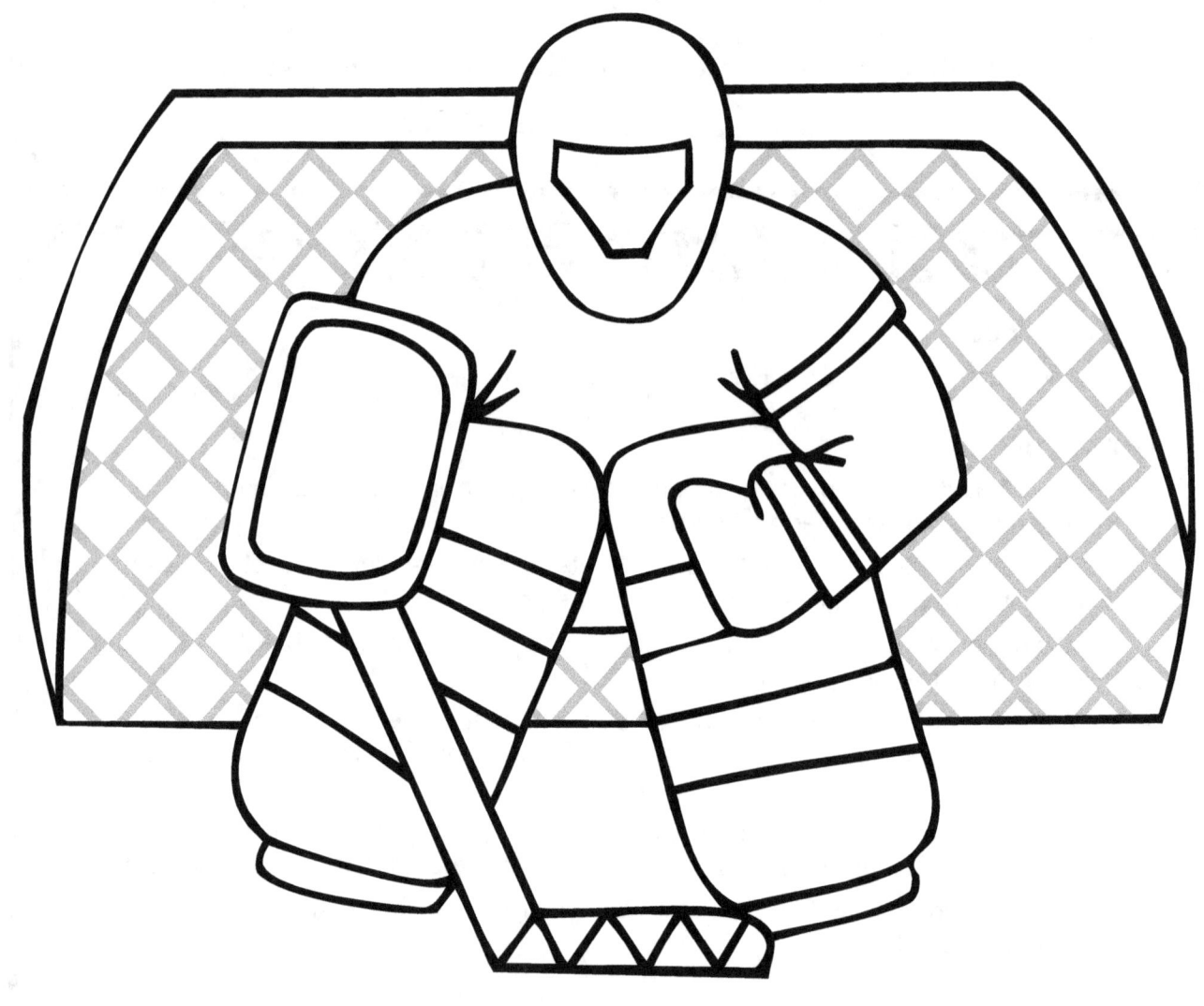

ELEMENTS OF DESIGN: SHAPE

Activity 1: Shape Picture

What you need:

- Black construction paper • Scissors • Shape cutouts • Glue • Coloring materials

What to do:

1. Ask students to plan and compose a picture using their choice of shape cutouts on a black background. Have available white and colored cutouts of geometric shapes. (You will find outlines of some geometric shapes on the following pages.) Possible subjects for students' pictures include animals, buildings, nature, people or inventions.

2. Once students have planned a detailed composition, have them glue the shapes onto the black construction paper. Encourage students to use a specific color scheme. Offer different media for coloring or adding designs to white cutouts.

Note: You may wish to demonstrate ways to use different shapes, for example, using heart shapes for an animal's feet.

Activity 2: Shape Collage

What you need:

- Paper
- Watercolors
- Paintbrushes
- Rulers
- Black markers
- Pencil

What to do:

1. Instruct students to produce a design of black outlines of overlapping geometric shapes. Encourage students to use a variety of shapes in their design.

2. Next, have students paint sections of the design using a specific approach such as complementary colors only, secondary colors only, different tints, and so on.

3. When students have finished, discuss with them their approach to their artwork.

SHAPE HUNT

Find and list places where you see or use the following geometric shapes in everyday life.

Circle

Octagon

Triangle

Trapezoid

Square

Hexagon

Rectangle

Oval

ORGANIC SHAPE HUNT

Organic Shape: Non-geometric or free-flowing shapes, such as a cloud or a leaf.

Look around you and draw different organic shapes you see.

HOW TO DRAW A DOG

Step 1

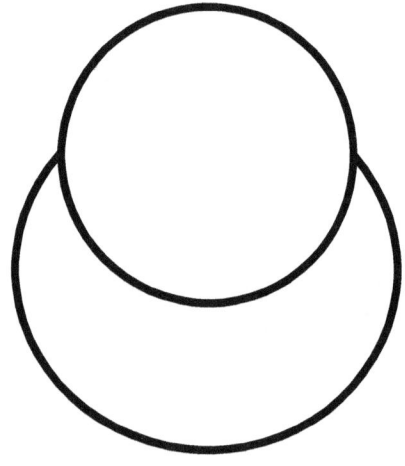

Step 2

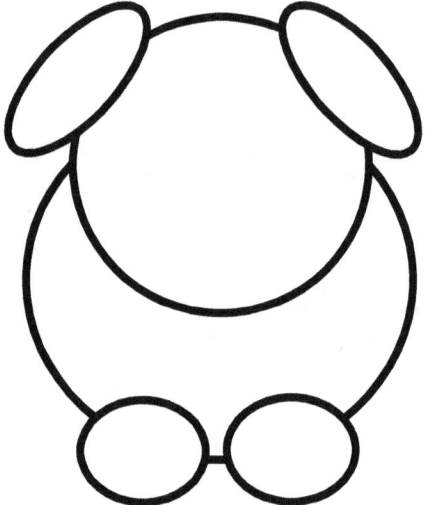

Step 3

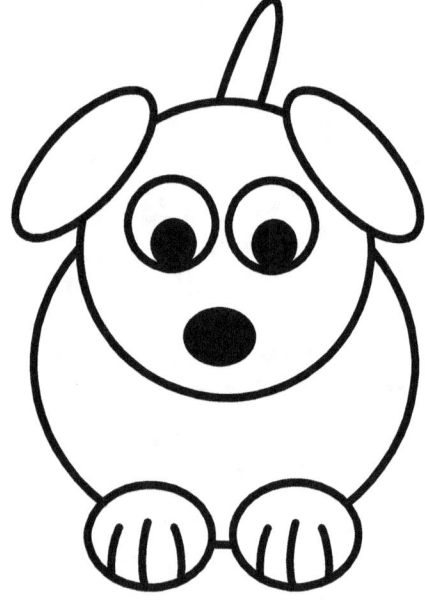

Step 4

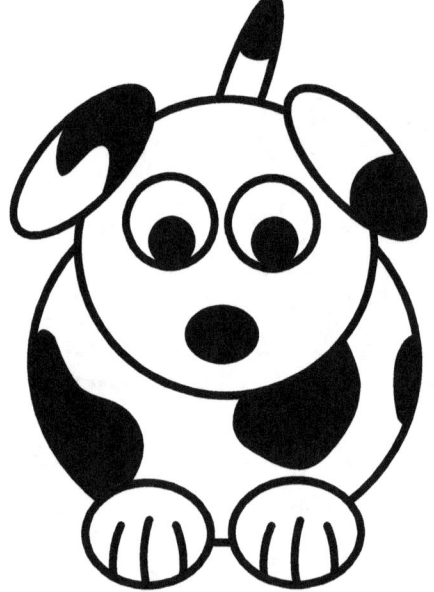

HOW TO DRAW A CAT

Step 1

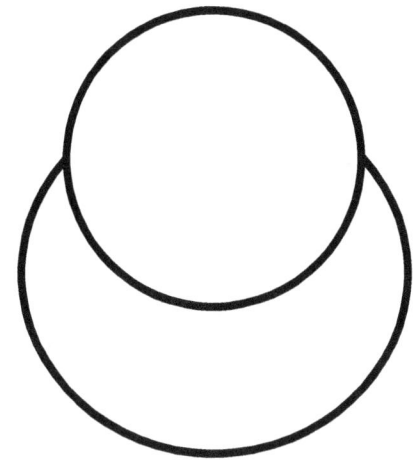

Step 2

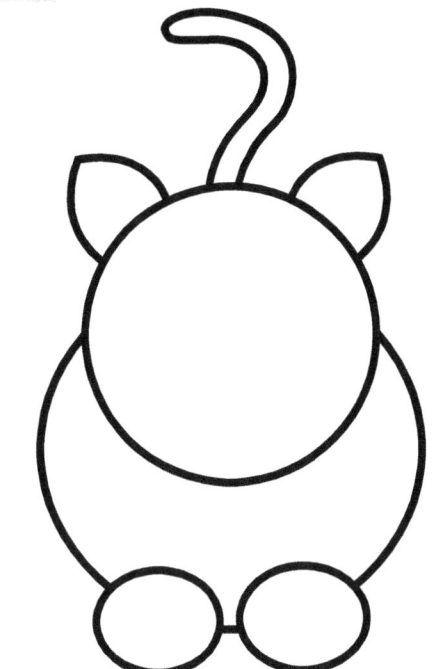

Step 3

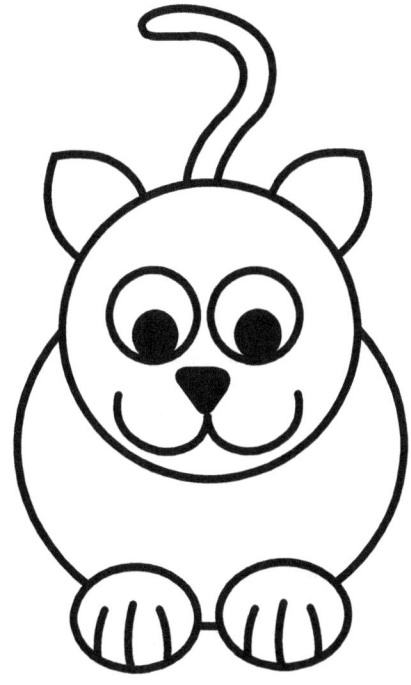

Step 4

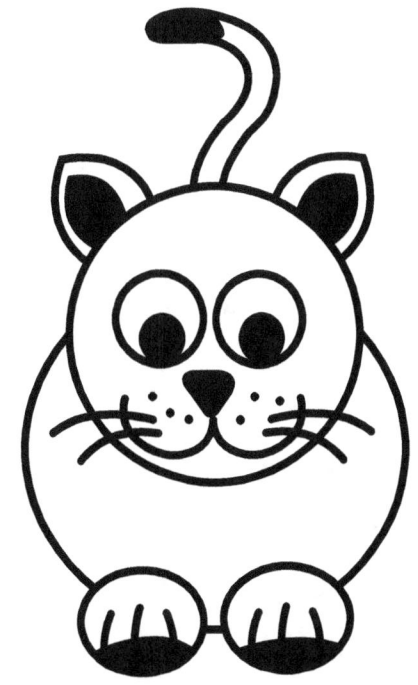

GEOMETRIC SHAPE OUTLINES

GEOMETRIC SHAPE OUTLINES

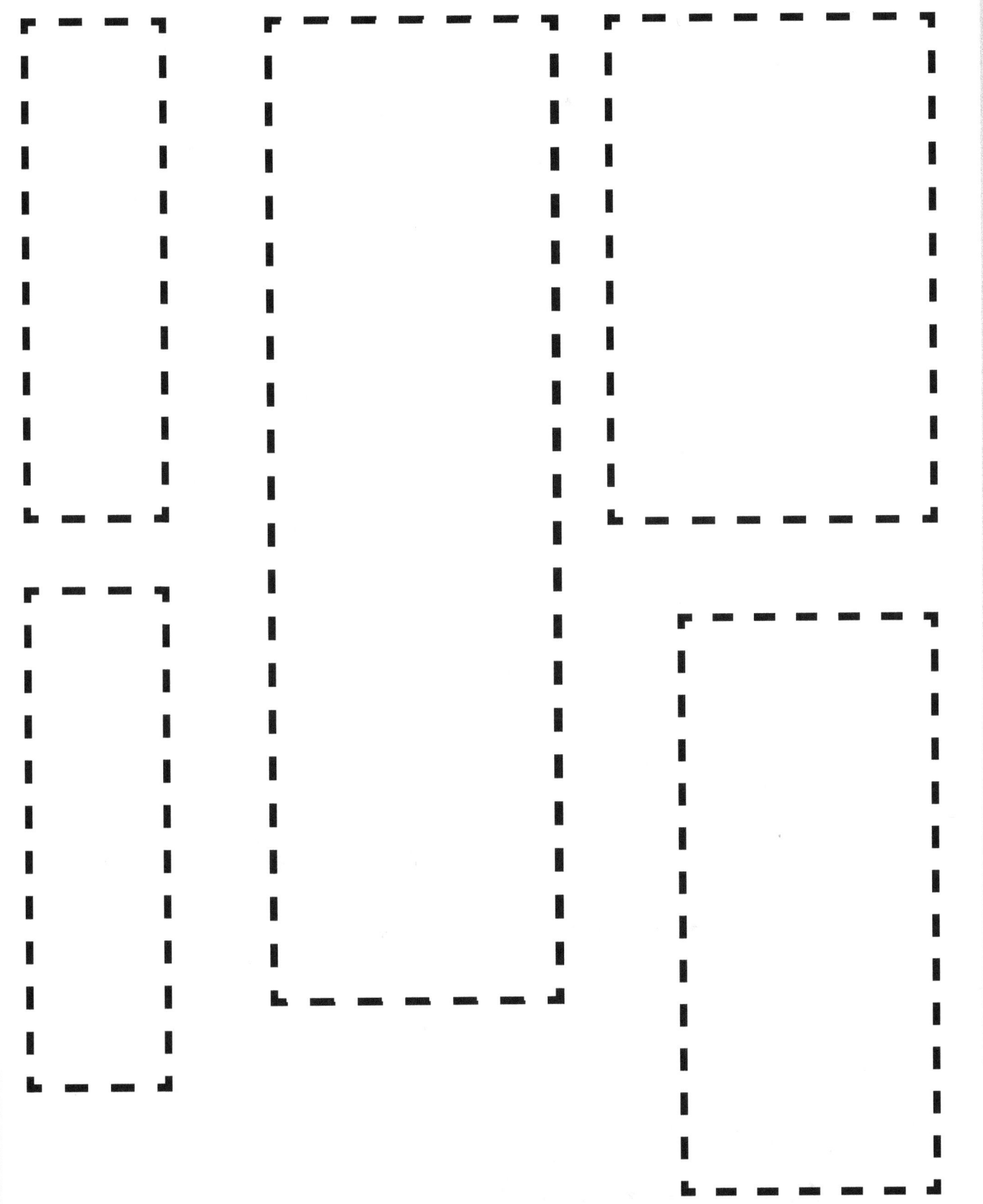

GEOMETRIC SHAPE OUTLINES

42

GEOMETRIC SHAPE OUTLINES

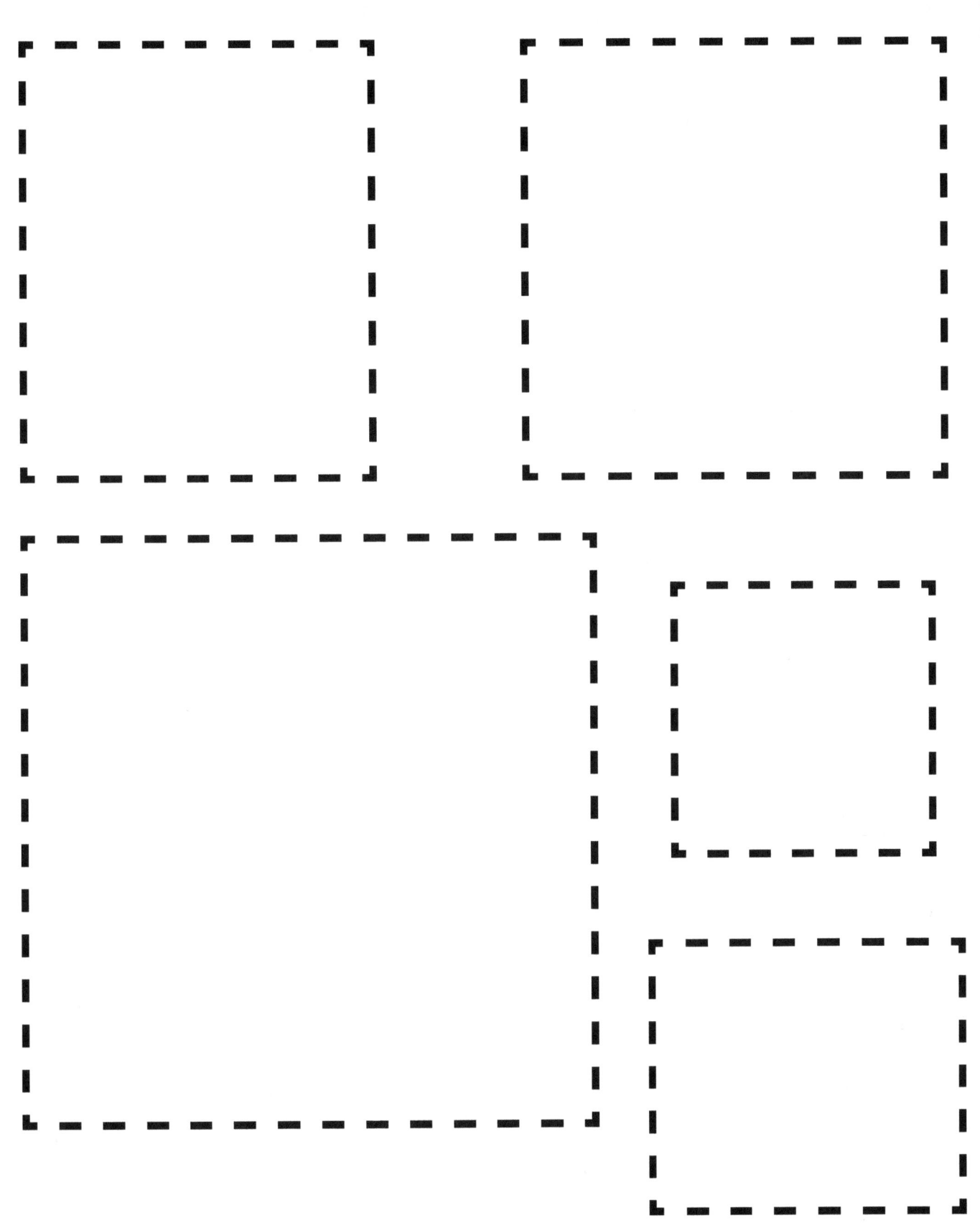

GEOMETRIC SHAPE OUTLINES

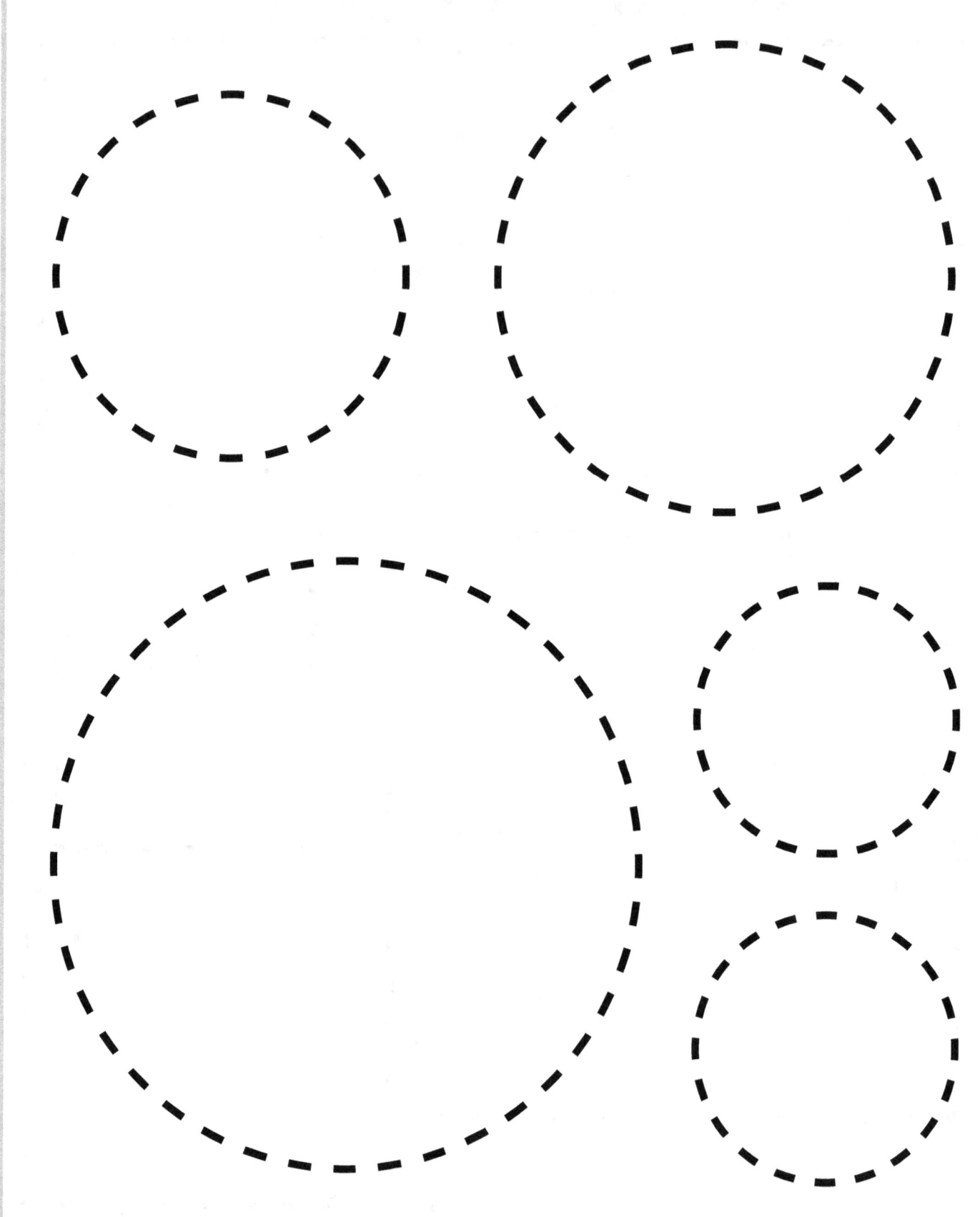

GEOMETRIC SHAPE OUTLINES

GEOMETRIC SHAPE OUTLINES

EXPERIMENTING WITH ELEMENTS OF DESIGN

Complete the picture using different elements of design. On a separate piece of paper, explain how you used the elements.

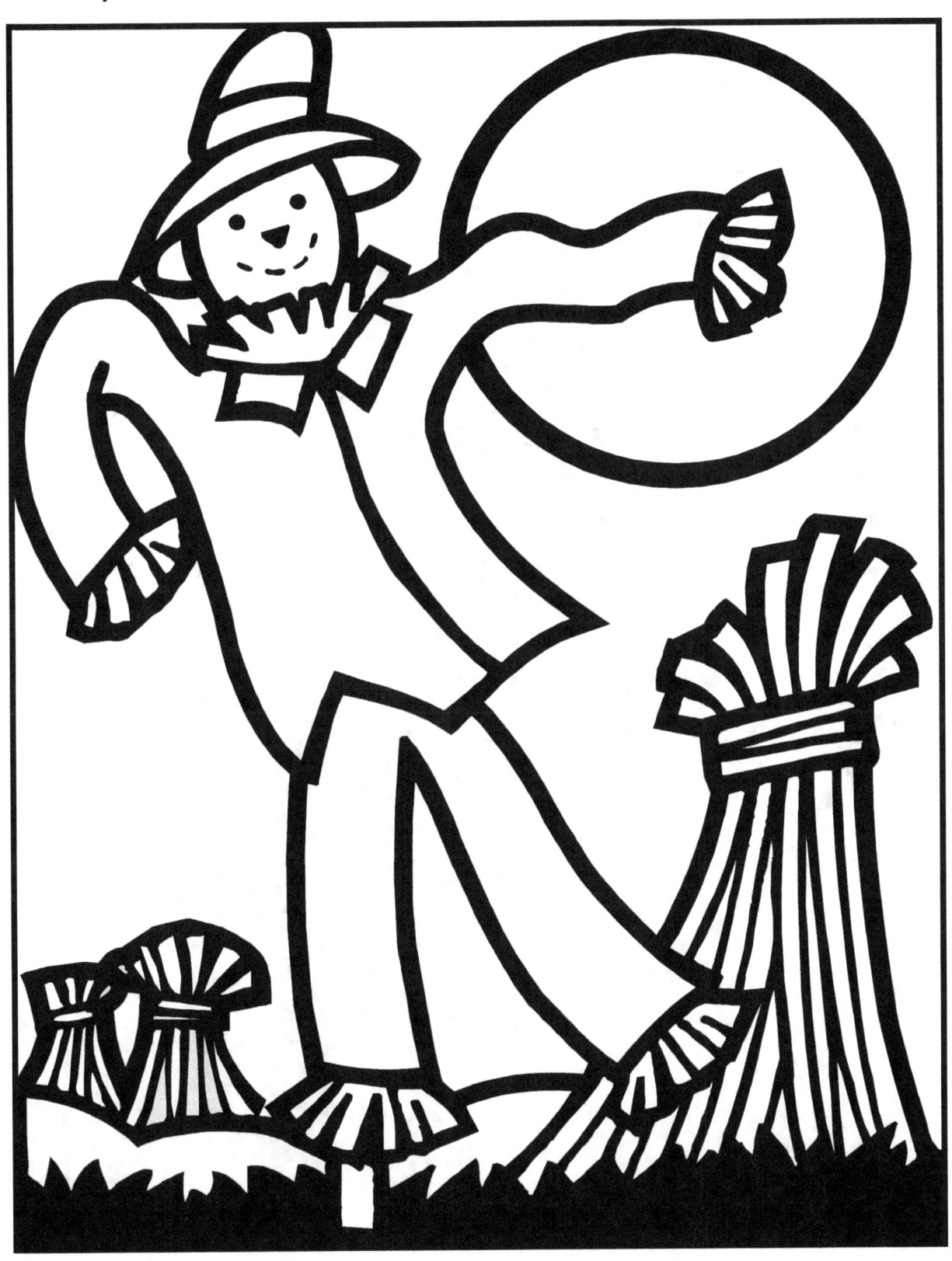

EXPERIMENTING WITH ELEMENTS OF DESIGN

Complete the picture using different elements of design. On a separate piece of paper, explain how you used the elements.

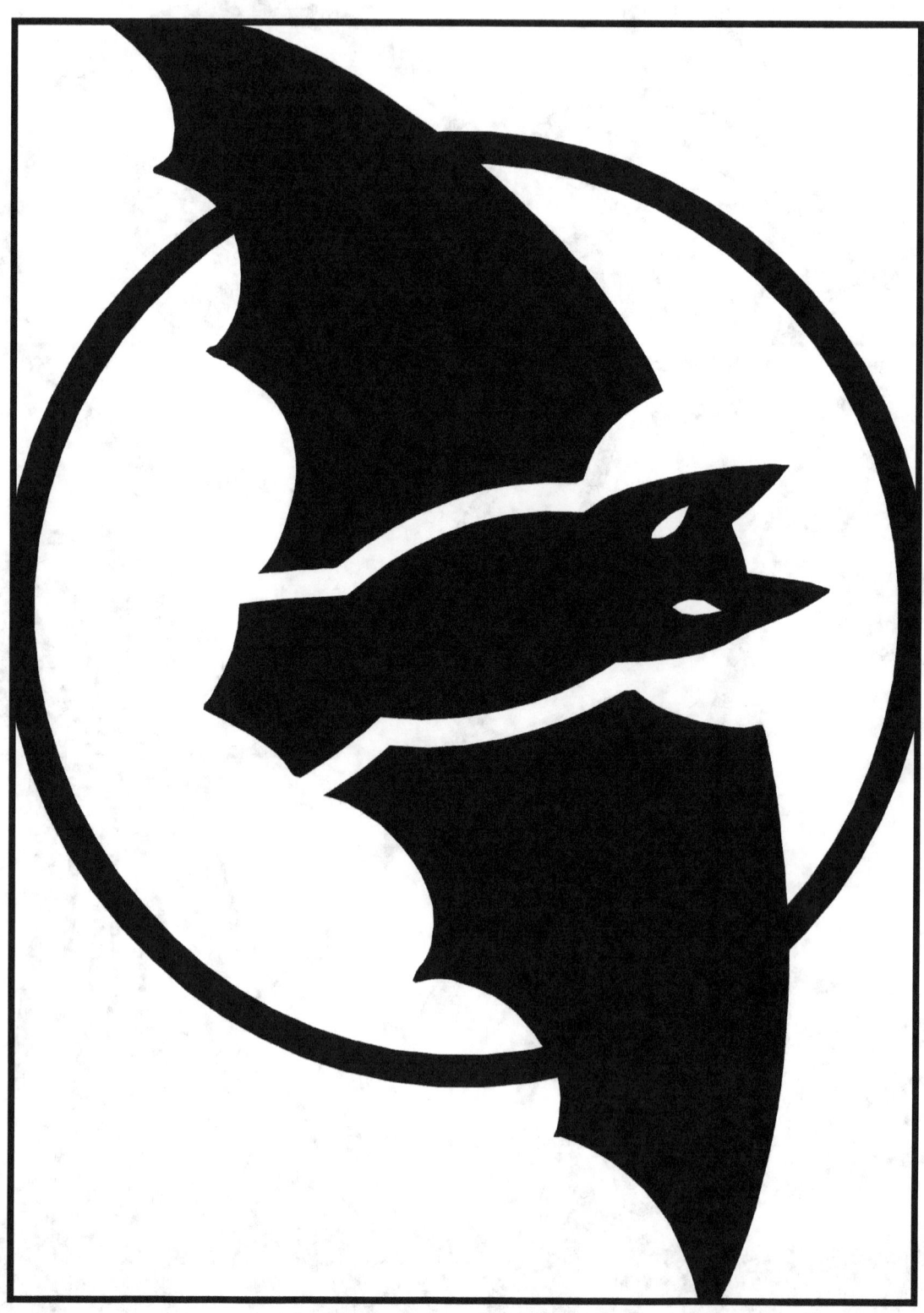

EXPERIMENTING WITH ELEMENTS OF DESIGN

Complete the picture using different elements of design. On a separate piece of paper, explain how you used the elements.

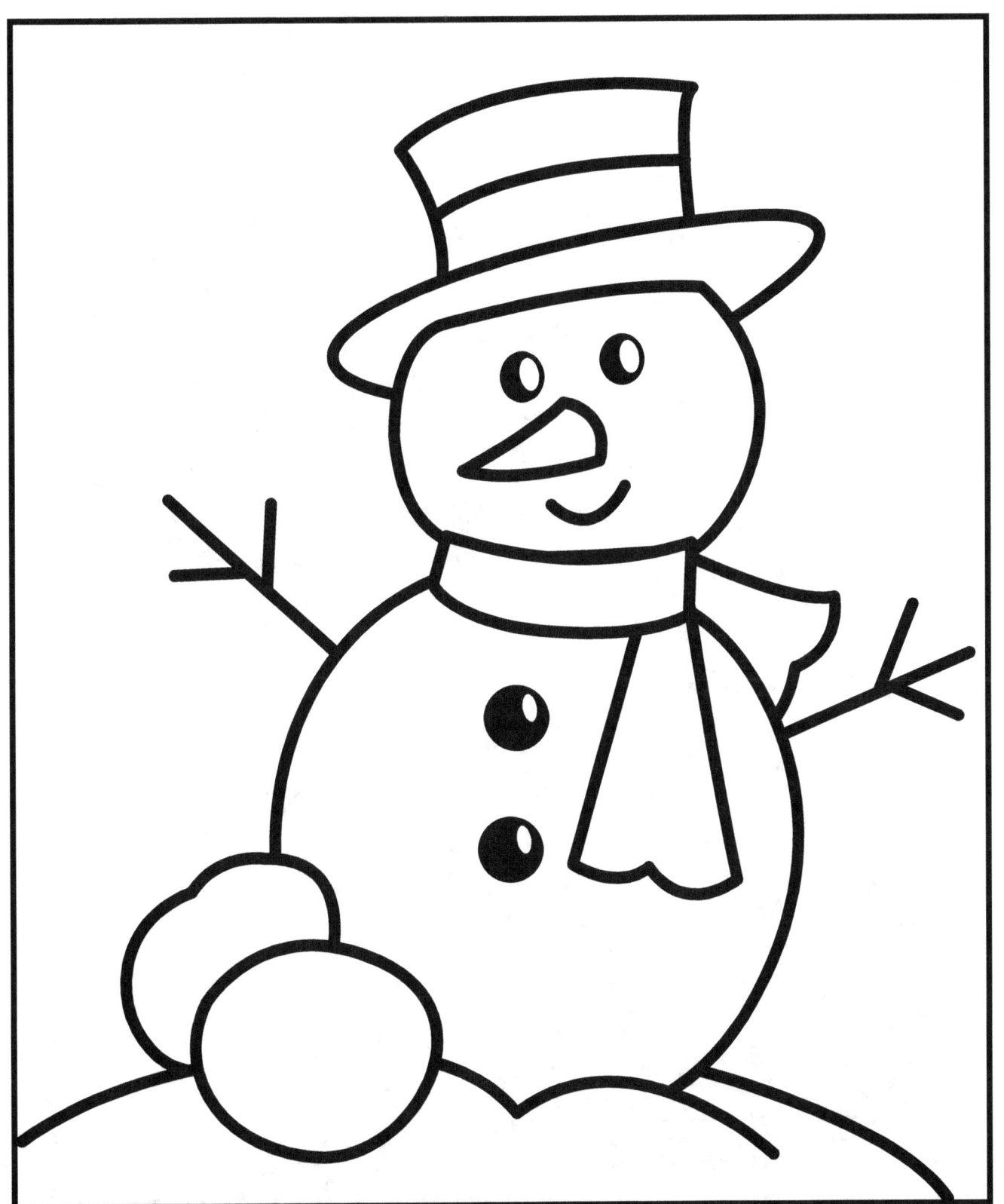

EXPERIMENTING WITH ELEMENTS OF DESIGN

Complete the picture using different elements of design. On a separate piece of paper, explain how you used the elements.

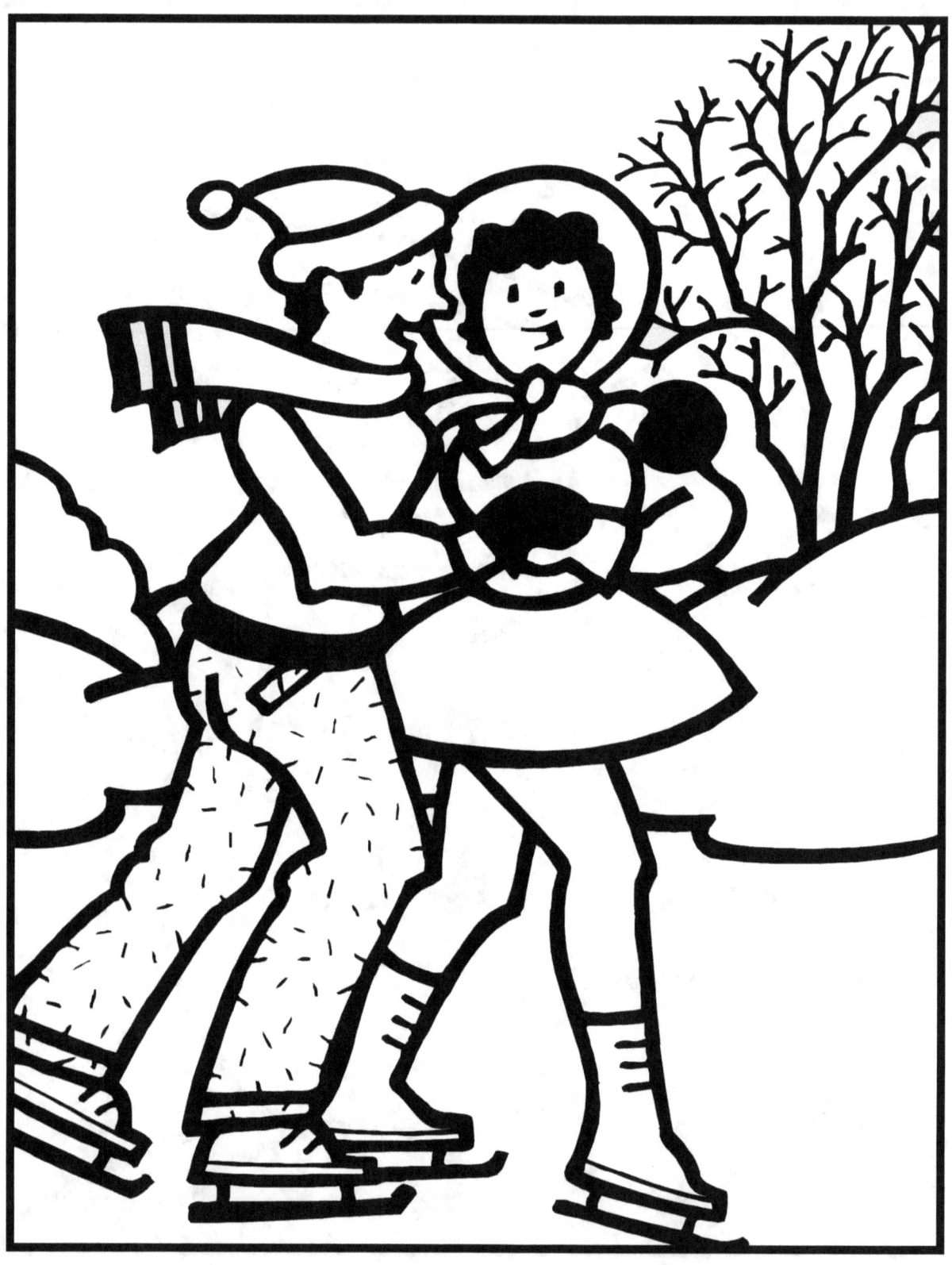

50

EXPERIMENTING WITH ELEMENTS OF DESIGN

Complete the picture using different elements of design. On a separate piece of paper, explain how you used the elements.

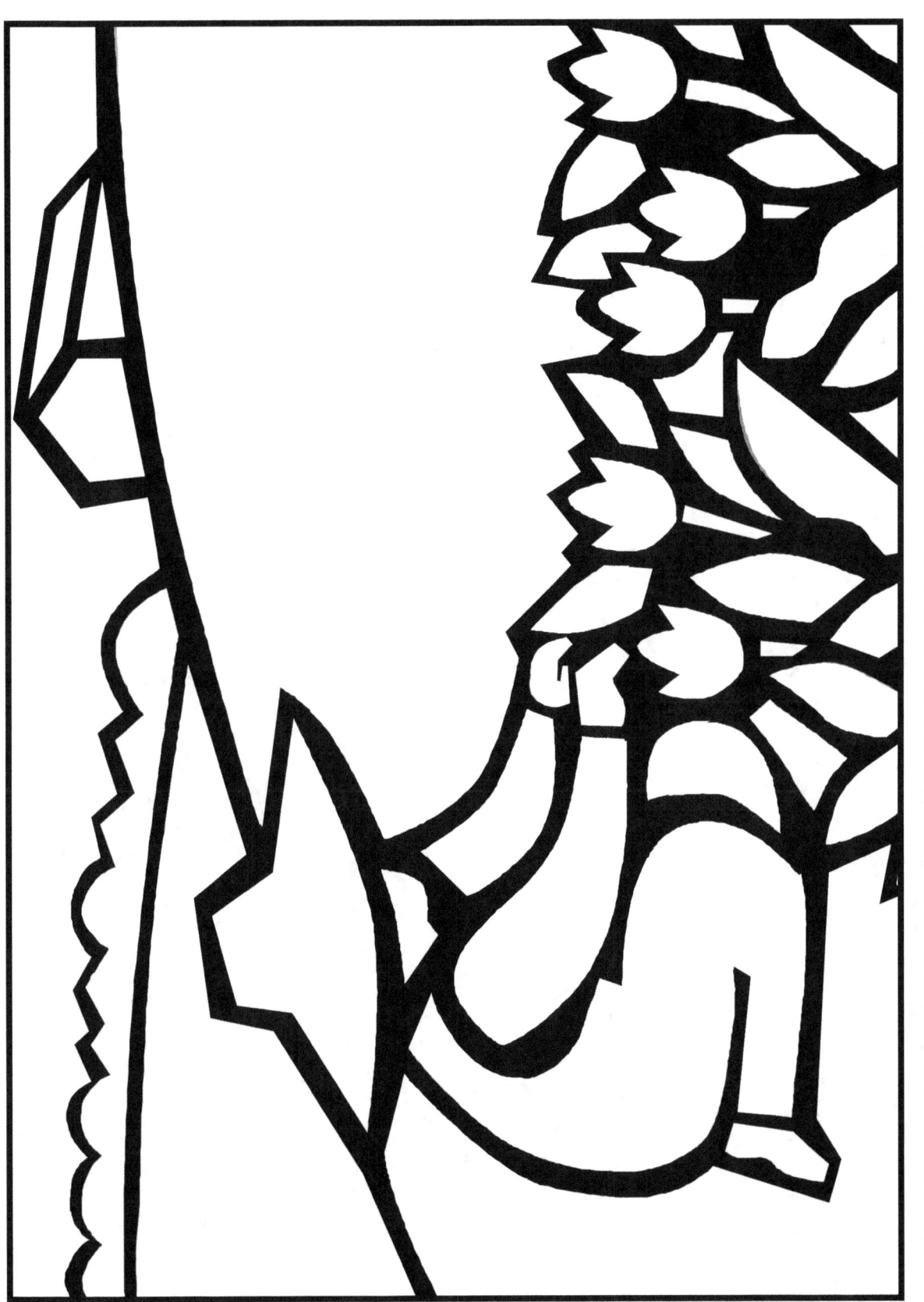

EXPERIMENTING WITH ELEMENTS OF DESIGN

Complete the picture using different elements of design. Make sure you add details to the background. On a separate piece of paper, explain how you used the elements.

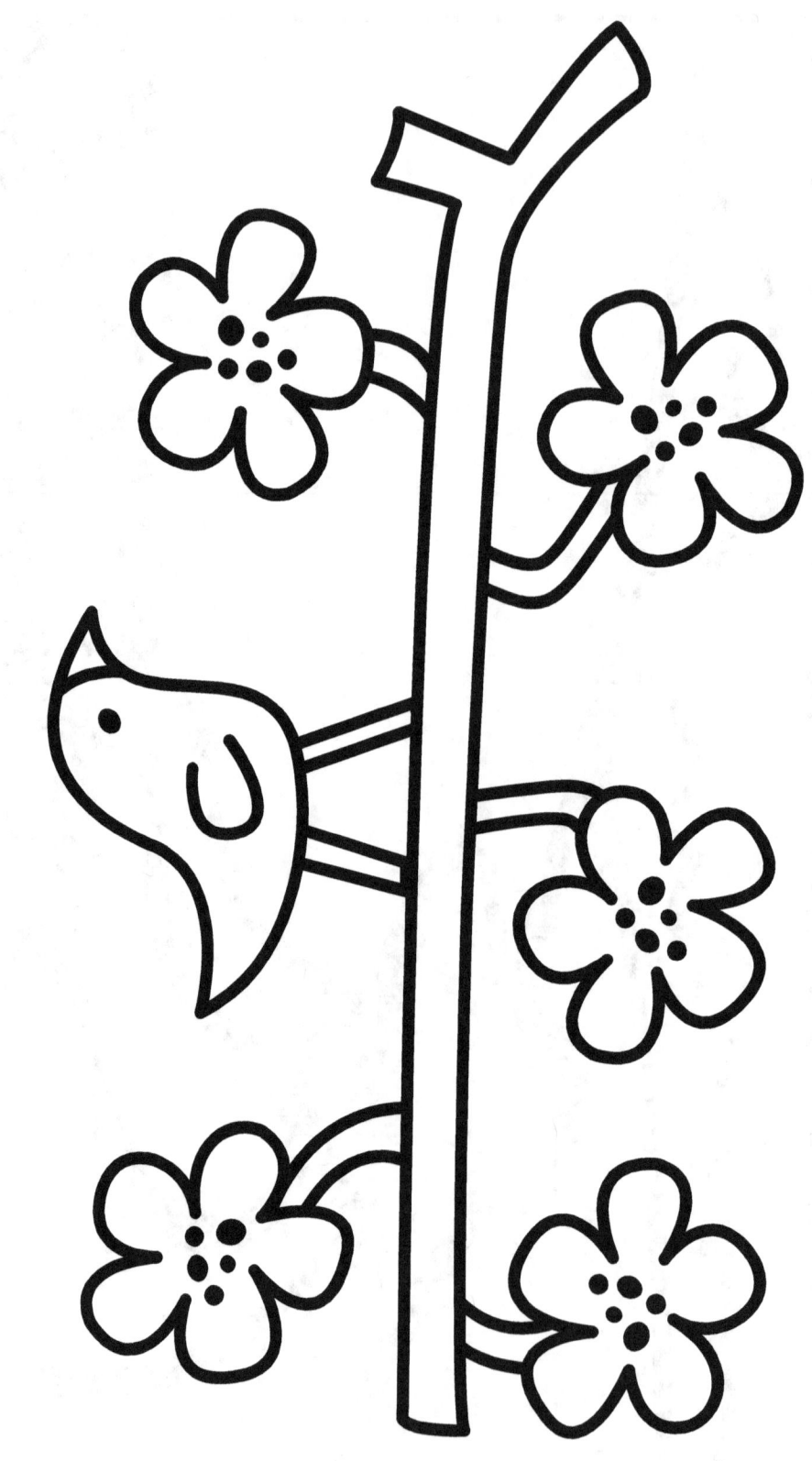

52

EXPERIMENTING WITH ELEMENTS OF DESIGN

Complete the picture using different elements of design. Make sure you add details to the background. On a separate piece of paper, explain how you used the elements.

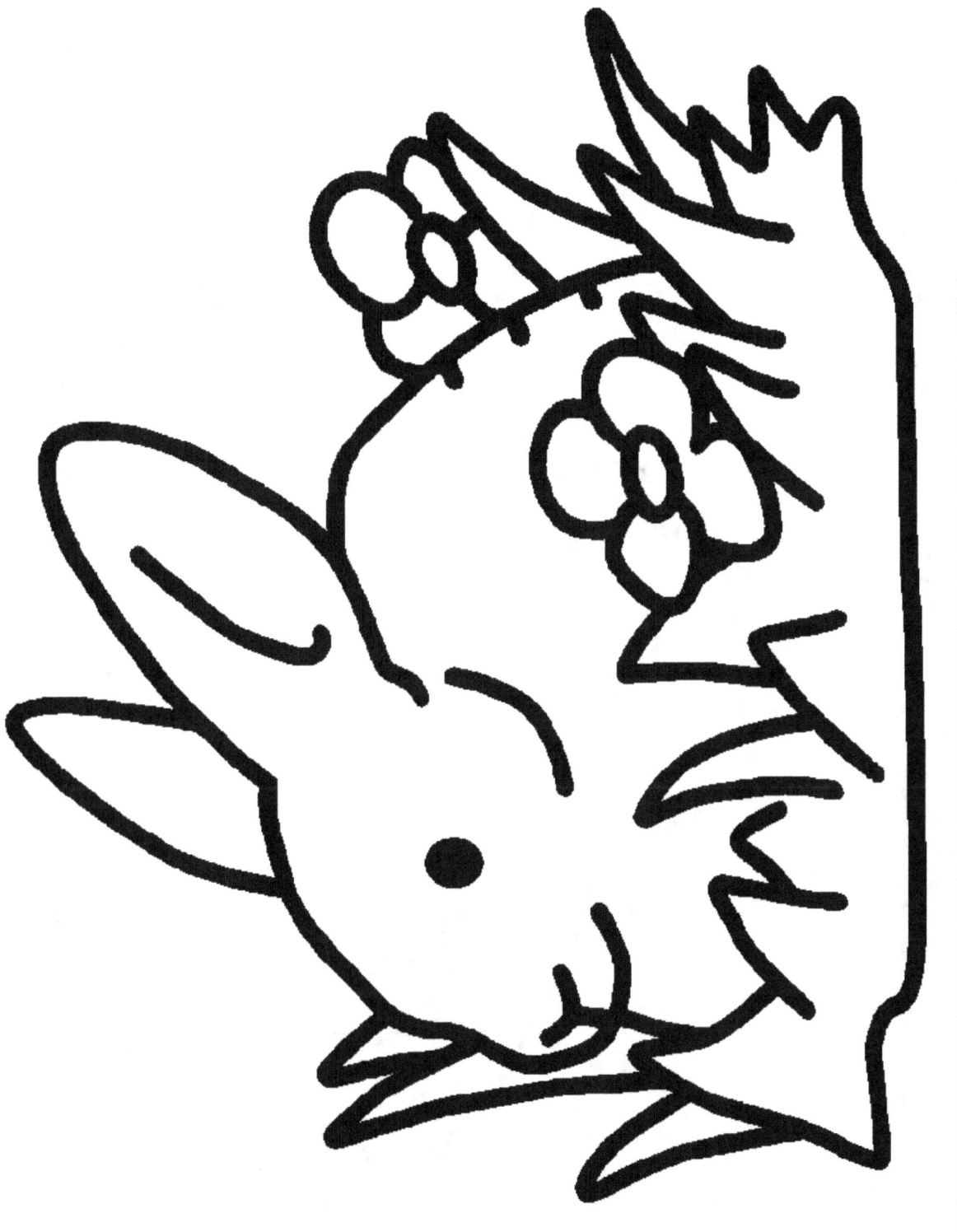

53
© Chalkboard Publishing

EXPERIMENTING WITH ELEMENTS OF DESIGN

Complete the picture using different elements of design. Make sure you add details to the background. On a separate piece of paper, explain how you used the elements.

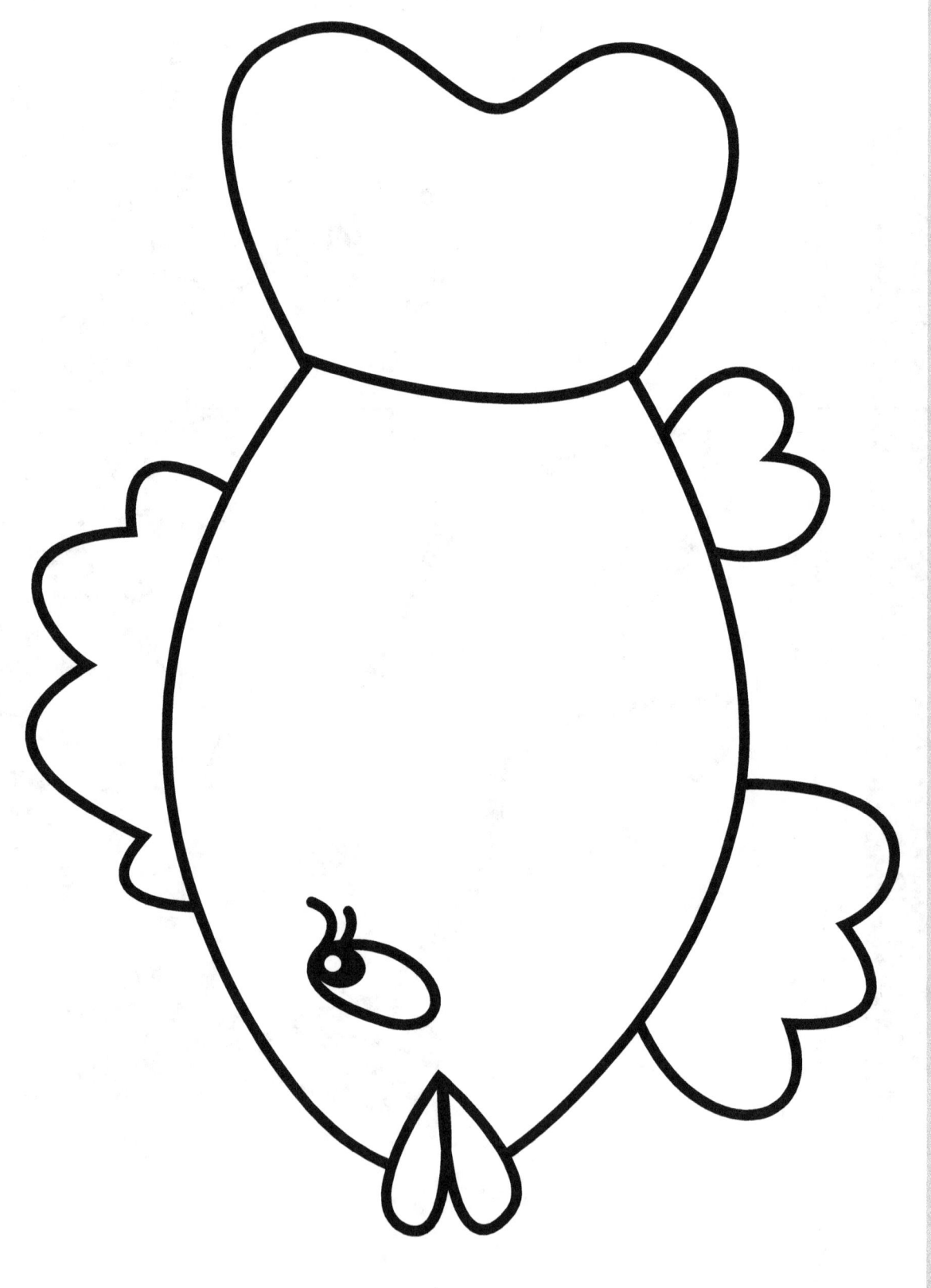

DRAW A PORTRAIT

Draw a family member, friend or pet.

CUTOUT ART

Create a picture using images cut out of old magazines.

COAT OF ARMS

Create your own coat of arms.

CREATE A STAMP

Create a stamp.

Write about your stamp:

_____

_____

_____

DISCUSSION PROMPTS: LOOKING AT A PAINTING

Description

- Describe the subject of the painting.
- What colors do you see?
- What shapes do you see?
- What textures do you see?
- What kind of lines do you see?
- What kind of objects do you see?
- What kind of forms do you see?

Analysis

- What is the focal point of the painting?
- Is there an element of design that is most prominent in the painting? Explain.
- Do you think the composition is balanced? Explain.
- Does the artist show movement in the painting? If so, how?
- Does the painting have a sense of three dimensions?
- What angle of view do you think the artist had when painting this subject? Explain your thinking.

Interpretation

- What kind of mood do you think the artist is trying to encourage when viewing the painting?
- How does the painting make you feel?
- What message or meaning do you think the artist is trying to convey?
- Why do you think the artist chose to paint this particular subject?

Personal Opinion

- Do you like the painting? Why or why not?
- What, if anything, does this painting remind you of? Explain.
- The painting is a good example of … or The painting is a bad example of …
- Do you think the title of the painting is a good one? Explain.
- Would you like to see more paintings from this artist? Why or why not?
- Would you buy this painting? Why or why not?

ARTIST-INSPIRED ART IDEAS

Jackson Pollock

What you need:

- Manila paper
- Plastic tub, large container or cardboard box
- Plastic squeeze bottles
- Various colors of paint
- Wooden craft sticks
- Music (optional)

What to do:

1. Explain to students that Jackson Pollock was an American artist known for a special abstract painting technique called "action painting." Most of his paintings did not feature any clear images, just dripped, sprayed and splattered paint.
2. Place the manila paper in the tub, container or box.
3. Model how to drip, spray or splatter paint from the plastic squeeze bottles in a controlled manner.
4. Play music to inspire students while they are painting. Students can change paint colors, the thickness of the drip, or the intensity of the splatter according to the music. For example, soft music could inspire long, sweeping motions or soft sprays of paint. Faster or dramatic music could inspire large splatters or short squirts of paint.
5. Encourage students to create interesting effects by moving a wooden craft stick through the paint in various ways.

American Collage

What you need:

- Glue
- Scissors
- White paper
- Magazine pictures
- American travel brochures

What to do:

1. Provide students with a variety of American magazines and travel brochures for vacation destinations in the United States. Ask students to search for and cut out pictures related to an American theme of their choice. Examples of themes include animals, plants, symbols, landscapes, vacation destinations, urban settings, or rural settings.
2. Have students arrange the pictures into a collage and paste them onto their paper.

ARTIST-INSPIRED ART IDEAS

Cityscape

What you need:
- Pictures of various cityscapes
- Black construction paper
- Newspapers
- Glue
- Rulers
- Scissors
- Pencils

What to do:
1. Display pictures of cityscapes for students to view. Point out that, from a distance, a group of buildings can look like blocks standing on end. Discuss as a class.
2. Draw a variety of horizons on the board. Discuss with students what "horizon" means.
3. Use a ruler to model creating a horizon line on a piece of black construction paper.
4. Model how to carefully cut out the columns of text in a newspaper. Students will glue the newspaper columns on the construction paper to make buildings in a cityscape.
5. Distribute the materials and have students create a cityscape.

Forest Landscape

What you need:
- Blue construction paper
- Magazine pictures of forest animals
- Glue
- Green tissue paper in a variety of shades
- Brown construction paper in a variety of shades

What to do:
1. Display for students photographs of forest landscapes and landscapes painted by various artists.
2. Demonstrate how to tear different lengths of brown construction paper to create tree trunks. Encourage students to add branches to their tree trunks.
3. Instruct students to glue the tree trunks and branches onto the blue paper. Remind them that smaller trees look as though they are located farther away.
4. Tear different shades of green tissue paper into small pieces to create leaves.
5. Have students paste the tissue paper leaves onto the tree branches and the forest floor.
6. Encourage students to paste cutout pictures of forest animals onto their picture for more detail.

ARTIST-INSPIRED ART IDEAS

Georgia O'Keeffe

What you need:

- White drawing paper
- Permanent black markers
- Watercolors or tempera paints

What to do:

1. Explain to students that Georgia O'Keeffe created abstract paintings of a wide variety of subjects, including still lifes, rocks, flowers, shells, landscapes and animal skulls.
2. Display several of Georgia O'Keeffe's flower paintings. Discuss each painting as a class.
3. Use a permanent black marker to model drawing an abstract flower on white paper. Start by drawing a circle on the top third of the paper. Around that circle, draw abstract petals in a circular scalloped pattern. Follow the outline of the petals to draw two more scalloped circles, each one larger than the last.
4. Draw a stem consisting of four or five vertical wavy lines spaced a little apart from each other. Draw each line from the bottom of the flower to the bottom of the paper.
5. Draw two small, thin leaves, one on each side of the stem. Draw several outlines around each leaf, making each one larger than the last.
6. Draw more scalloped lines for the flower and outlines for the leaves until the paper has been completely filled. The drawing will look as though it extends past the paper.
7. Have students draw an abstract flower following your example. Note: You may choose to have students complete each step of the process immediately following the demonstration.

Native American Beadwork Design

What you need:

- Graph paper, 10 squares × 50 squares
- Various colors of markers
- Examples or pictures of Native American beadwork

What to do:

1. Display examples or pictures of Native American beadwork, such as from the Great Plains tribes, for students to view. Explain to students that this is a traditional Native American art form.
2. Distribute graph paper to each student.
3. Model how to create a design on graph paper, such as a bird, tree, or a traditional Native American design. To provide students with inspiration for their designs, you may wish to read with the class several Native American stories and legends.
4. Have students draw and color their design.

DESIGN YOUR OWN OLYMPIC MEDAL

Look at pictures of the medals handed out at past Olympic Games. Then design your own medal!

- Consider different elements of design, such as form, texture and shape.
- Think about the size of your medal, what it will be made of, and how an athlete will wear it.

GREAT SEAL OF THE UNITED STATES

Color the Great Seal of the United States.

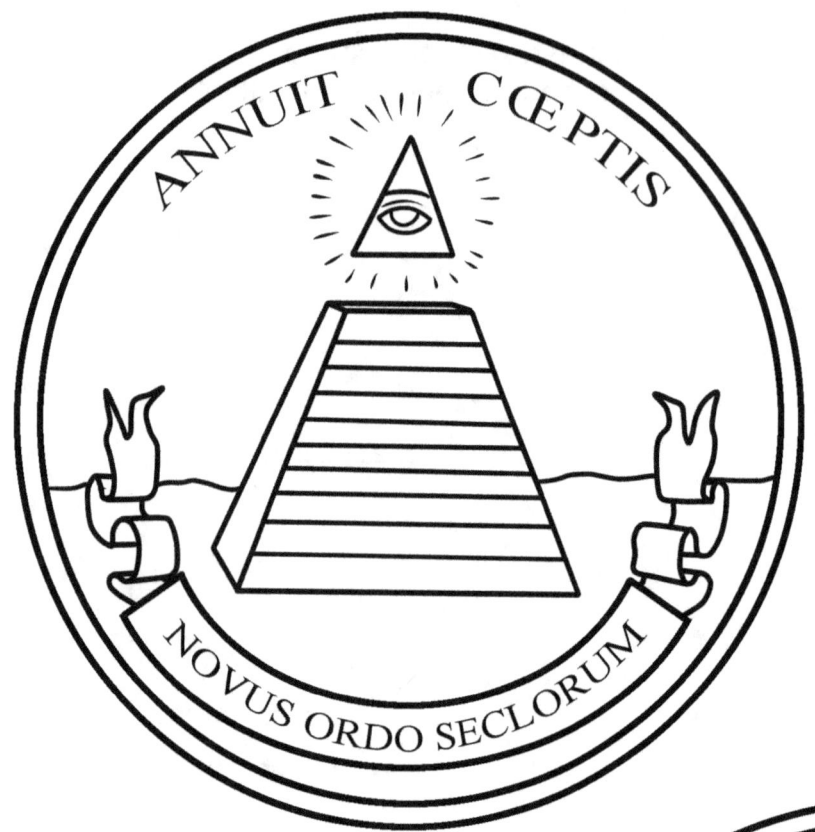

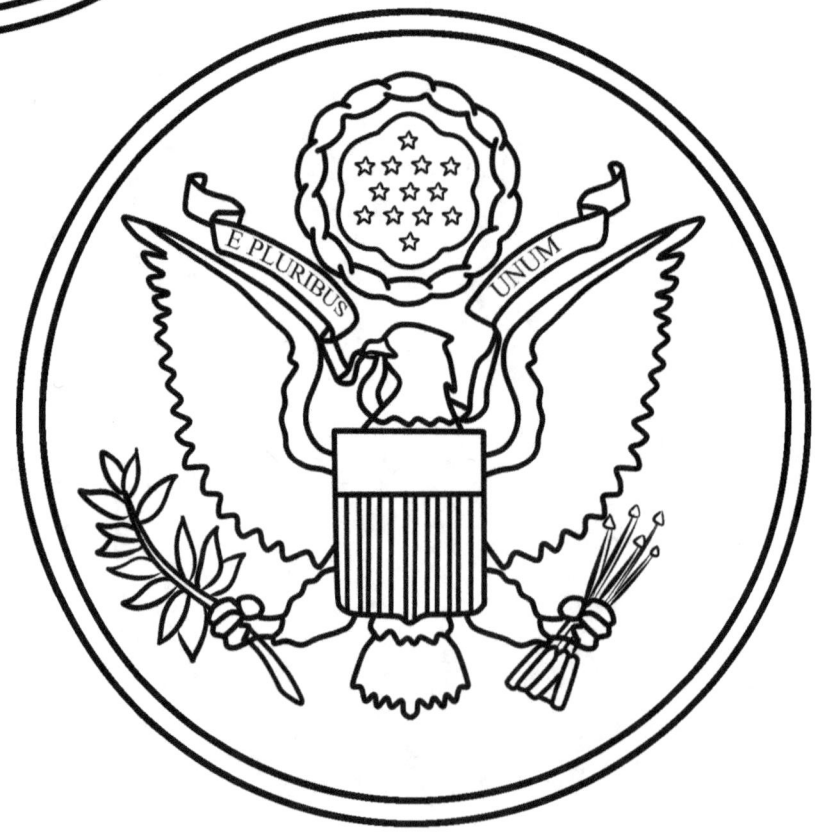

SIMILARITIES AND DIFFERENCES

Describe two artworks.

Artist and description of artwork

Artist and description of artwork

Compare

How are the artworks **similar**?

_____
_____
_____
_____

Contrast

How are the artworks **different**?

_____
_____
_____
_____

DIRECT DRAW

Encourage students to think of art as the personal interpretation of ideas. This quick activity demonstrates how students given the same directions will each produce a unique artwork. Collect and display all of the students' completed artworks. You will have a wonderful collection of abstract art based on shape, color and line.

WHAT YOU NEED:

- piece of square paper
- coloring materials

WHAT TO DO:

1. Tell students that they will each complete a piece of art by following your oral directions. Before you begin, ask students to predict whether or not all the students' works will look the same.

2. Give each student the same materials.

3. Call out directions. For example:
   - Draw a thin line across the page.
   - Draw a thick line across the page.
   - Draw a circle anywhere on the page.
   - Draw a triangle somewhere on the page.
   - ...

   Add directions of your choice that will reinforce art vocabulary. Give students enough time to follow each direction before calling out the next one.

4. When all the directions have been called out, have students compare and contrast their artworks with a partner. How are the pieces the same? How are they different?

5. Display the students' artworks.

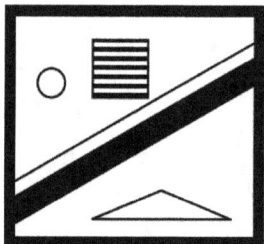 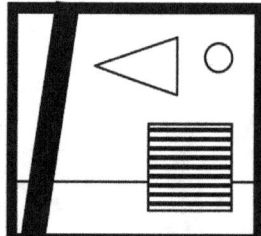 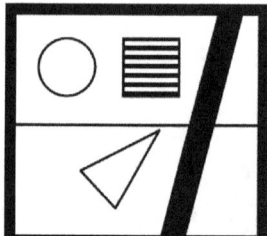 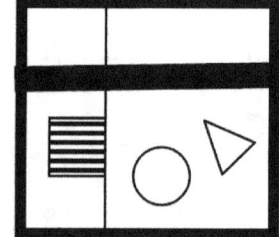

SKETCHBOOK DRAWING IDEAS

Portrait

- Draw a self-portrait. Look at yourself in a mirror for reference.
- Draw a self-portrait of yourself 50 years from now.
- Draw a portrait of a friend or family member.
- Draw a portrait of your favorite stuffed animal.
- Draw a portrait of your pet.
- Draw a portrait of your favorite cartoon character.

Still Life

- Draw a beautiful flower arrangement.
- Draw a plant with attention to detail.
- Draw a piece of fruit.
- Draw a piece of furniture with attention to color, shading and textures.
- Draw a favorite toy.
- Draw a bowl of fruit.
- Draw an arrangement of 3D figures with attention to shading.

Design

- Design a CD cover for your favorite group or singer.
- Design a logo for your class.
- Design a new cover for a book.
- Design an advertisement for a special event.
- Design a poster for your favorite movie.
- Design the can for a new drink.
- Design the outside of your dream house.
- Design a new invention.
- Design a new stamp.
- Design a new American coin.
- Design a new outfit.
- Design a car.
- Design a new American flag.
- Design a castle.

Other

- Draw a scene from another planet.
- Draw a giant looking down at a village.
- Draw a new creature.
- Draw an alien.
- Draw an airplane.
- Draw a spaceship.
- Draw what you see outside your bedroom window.
- Draw a boat.
- Draw what the world looked like during the time of the dinosaurs.

SEASONAL ART IDEAS

FALL

- Paint a fall mural on the classroom windows using a mixture of equal parts dishwashing liquid and paint (use washable liquid paint or powdered tempera paint). Encourage students to add as many details as possible.

- Make paper ears of corn. Students cut long ear-of-corn shapes from yellow construction paper. Instruct students to glue down small squares of yellow, orange and brown tissue paper to represent the kernels. When the glue is dry, add brown construction paper in the shape of the husk to the back.

- Sketch a still life of a cornucopia.

- Make leaf rubbings. Students should bring in fall leaves in all shapes and sizes and arrange them on paper. Students place another piece of paper on top and use chalk or crayons to make different types of rubbings.

- Use the shape outline cutouts in this resource to assemble shape pictures of a Halloween cat, witch, haunted house or bat. Students can paint the shapes using a textured paint and glue them onto black construction paper.

- Paint a spooky, black-and-orange Halloween picture.

- Assemble pasta skeletons. Provide students with different-shaped pieces of pasta and black construction paper. Students should glue the pasta pieces down once they are pleased with their arrangement.

- Produce beautiful "stained glass" Christmas windows using black construction paper and tissue paper. Students cut out Christmas symbols from the black construction paper, leaving the "window frame." Then students carefully paste different colors of tissue paper to create a stained glass effect.

- Construct three-dimensional Christmas trees. First, tell students to fold two rectangular pieces of green construction paper in half. Then, show students how to do the following: draw half a Christmas tree opposite the fold on one piece of paper, place the folded pieces of paper one on top of the other, and cut along the outline of the tree to produce two identical, symmetrical tree shapes. Cut a slit along the crease in the center of the bottom half of one tree and the top half of the other tree. Fit the two shapes together.

SEASONAL ART IDEAS

WINTER

- Paint a winter mural on the classroom windows using a mixture of equal parts dishwashing liquid and paint (use washable liquid paint or powdered tempera paint).

- Draw a winter scene using crayons and apply a wash with salt added, for a snowy effect.

- Draw people in motion participating in various winter sports and activities.

- Make Valentine's Day pendants using self-hardening clay. Students can mold their own shape or use cookie cutters as guides. Paint the pendants with acrylic paint once the clay is dry.

- Weave a paper heart. Model for students how to fold a piece of red or pink construction paper exactly in half. Then, using a pencil, draw the outline of half a heart opposite the fold and cut along the outline to create a heart shape. Demonstrate for students how to carefully cut long slits parallel to the fold without cutting the heart into pieces. Then show them how to weave strips of white, red and pink paper through the heart.

- Create a shamrock crown. Students cut shamrock shapes in different sizes and sponge paint them in different tints and shades of green. Once the shamrocks are dry, students paste them onto a strip of green construction paper. Staple the strip to fit each student's head. Students could also glitter to their crowns.

- Go outside on a snowy day and create snow sculptures!

- Make glossy snowflakes. Students cut snowflakes out of aluminum foil and carefully paste white tissue paper behind them. Display the snowflakes on a window.

SEASONAL ART IDEAS

 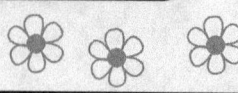

SPRING

- Paint a spring mural on the classroom windows using a mixture of equal parts dishwashing liquid and paint (use washable liquid paint or powdered tempera paint).

- Create seed mosaics using the shape outlines in this book as a base.

- Paper-mache old vases in spring colors. Students can plant a flower in the vase (or fill it with paper flowers) and give it as a Mother's Day gift.

- Decorate the classroom with gorgeous spring blossoms. First, students paint brown branches on white paper. When the paint is dry, they add tissue paper blossoms as follows: wrap small squares of tissue paper around the end of a pencil, dab on a small amount of glue, and paste each square onto a branch.

- Use oil pastels to draw and color realistic pictures of spring flowers or insects. Students should use close-up photographs as references. Set students' pictures with hair spray.

- Draw a still life of an Easter lily arrangement

- Design an Earth Day stamp or commemorative coin.

- Create an Earth Day collage using cutouts from old magazines and other print media.

- Decorate paper Easter eggs. Students cut egg shapes out of construction paper and draw line patterns on them with water-based markers. Students can trace over the marker lines with white glue to produce an embossed effect (the glue will dry clear).

- Produce beautiful insect and flower "stained glass" windows using black construction paper and tissue paper. Students cut out the desired shapes from the black construction paper, leaving the "window frame." Then students carefully paste different colors of tissue paper to create a stained glass effect.

- Make colorful paper-bag birds. Students start by cutting feathers of different shapes and sizes from construction paper. Demonstrate how to place and glue the feathers around the bag, starting from the back. Encourage students to create a pattern of color. Students can add triangle-shaped wings covered in feathers, eyes, and a beak.

SEASONAL ART IDEAS

SUMMER

- Paint a summer mural on the classroom windows using a mixture of equal parts dishwashing liquid and paint (use washable liquid paint or powdered tempera paint).

- Make miniature kites. Use straws or wooden craft sticks to construct the frame and cover it with tissue paper. Attach string.

- Create beautiful tissue paper flowers. Students take four to six rectangular pieces of tissue paper and fold them as a pile into an accordion. Next, they tie the center of the pile with a twist tie. Demonstrate for students how to carefully pull each piece of tissue paper up toward the center of the flower, so that the pieces of tissue paper are separated to form petals. Finally, add a stem using a green pipe cleaner or Bristol board.

- Celebrate Independence Day. Design a stamp using the blackline master in this resource and/or create a diorama depicting all things American.

- Turn a rock into a paperweight and give it as a gift for Father's Day. Invite students to bring rocks to class and to decorate the rock of their choice with acrylic paint.

- Draw the outline of a summer scene and fill sections of the drawing using mixed media.

- Draw a still life of beach toys, your favorite place to visit during the summer, or a bicycle.

- Use oil pastels to draw a still life of a bowl of fruit.

- Build a sandcastle using sand clay. Once the sandcastle is finished, students should gently pat dry sand on the moist clay.

- Create a diorama of a summer garden or a beach scene.

- Design and create a mixed-media poster of the ultimate vacation spot. Students can use magazine pictures of places they would like to visit for inspiration and reference.

- Assemble two-dimensional paper flowers with stems and leaves. Students can arrange cutout shapes (from the shape outline blackline masters) on a colored piece of construction paper and fill in each shape with a textured paint.

ART RUBRICS

UNDERSTANDING OF ART CONCEPTS RUBRIC

LEVEL	DESCRIPTORS
4	Student shows a thorough understanding of all or almost all concepts and consistently gives appropriate and complete explanations independently. No teacher support is needed.
3	Student shows a good understanding of most concepts and usually gives complete or nearly complete explanations. Infrequent teacher support is needed.
2	Student shows a satisfactory understanding of most concepts and sometimes gives appropriate, but incomplete, explanations. Teacher support is sometimes needed.
1	Student shows little understanding of concepts and rarely gives complete explanations. Intensive teacher support is needed.

COMMUNICATION OF CONCEPTS RUBRIC

LEVEL	DESCRIPTORS
4	Student almost always uses correct art terminology with clarity and precision during class discussions.
3	Student frequently uses correct art terminology during class discussions.
2	Student occasionally uses correct art terminology during class discussions.
1	Student rarely uses correct art terminology during class discussions.

ART RUBRICS

ANALYSIS OF ARTWORKS RUBRIC

LEVEL	DESCRIPTORS
4	Student accurately describes several dominant elements or principles used by the artist. Student accurately describes how they are used by the artist to reinforce the theme, meaning, mood or feeling of the artwork.
3	Student describes without assistance most of the dominant elements and principles used by the artist. Student describes without assistance how these relate to the meaning, mood, theme or feeling of the artwork.
2	Student describes with little assistance some dominant elements and principles used by the artist. Student needs some teacher prompts to describe how these relate to the meaning, mood, theme or feeling of the artwork.
1	Student has difficulty describing the dominant elements and principles used by the artist in the artwork without direct teacher prompts.

INTERPRETATION OF ARTWORKS RUBRIC

LEVEL	DESCRIPTORS
4	Student analyzes and interprets the meaning of the artwork independently using extensive evidence from the artwork.
3	Student analyzes and interprets the meaning of the artwork with occasional teacher prompts using satisfactory evidence from the artwork.
2	Student requires some teacher prompts to analyze and interpret the meaning of the artwork.
1	Student requires direct teacher assistance to analyze and interpret the meaning of the artwork.

ART RUBRICS

CREATIVE WORK RUBRIC

LEVEL	DESCRIPTORS
4	Student applies almost all of the skills, techniques and art concepts taught.
3	Student applies most of the skills, techniques and art concepts taught.
2	Student applies more than half of the skills, techniques and art concepts taught.
1	Student applies fewer than half of the skills, techniques and art concepts taught.

PARTICIPATION RUBRIC

LEVEL	DESCRIPTORS
4	Student consistently contributes to class discussions and activities by offering ideas and asking questions.
3	Student usually contributes to class discussions and activities by offering ideas and asking questions.
2	Student sometimes contributes to class discussions and activities by offering ideas and asking questions.
1	Student rarely contributes to class discussions and activities by offering ideas and asking questions.

© Chalkboard Publishing

CLASS EVALUATION LIST

Student Name	Class Participation	Understanding of Concepts	Communication of Concepts	Analysis of Artworks	Interpretation of Artworks	Creative Work	Overall Evaluation

© Chalkboard Publishing

ART WEB SITES FOR STUDENTS

Hello Kids

http://www.hellokids.com/

Have students visit the "Drawing" section of this fantastic site. Here students will find several easy-to-follow, step-by-step instructions for drawing a variety of animals and characters.

Learn About Color

http://www.metmuseum.org/metmedia/interactives/start-with-art/learn-about-color

Here, students can mix colors and watch as a labeled color wheel is assembled.

Smithsonian American Art Museum

http://americanart.si.edu/education/resources/activities/index.cfm

The "Education" page of the museum's Web site offers links to student activities, including "Zoom It," which allows students to zoom in for a closer look at various areas in a number of works of art.

Metropolitan Museum of Art—Kids' Zone

http://www.metmuseum.org/metmedia/kids-zone

Interactive activities and podcasts about art, artists, and world cultures, particularly those featured in the collections of the Met.

The National Gallery of Art

http://www.nga.gov/education/index.shtm

The gallery's Web site offers this "Education" page. Explore with students the following links on the page: NGA Classroom: Online Resources for Teachers and Students; NGA Kids; Children's Video Tour.

Build Your Wild Self

http://buildyourwildself.com/

This is a great Web site where students can design a digital human and add animal characteristics.

ART GLOSSARY

Abstract art: Art that uses lines, shapes, colors and textures to portray a realistic object in a non-realistic, imaginary way.

Allegory: The use of symbolic figures to represent abstract ideas such as honor and sacrifice.

Analogous colors: Two or more colors that are next to each other on the color wheel. For example: red, red-orange and orange.

Background: The part of the picture plane that seems to be farthest from the viewer.

Balance: A principle of design that deals with arranging the visual elements in a work of art for harmony of design and proportion.

Cast shadow: The shadow created on a surface when an objects blocks the light.

Complementary colors: Colors opposite each other on the color wheel. For example: yellow and purple.

Collage: Creating a picture by gluing pieces of materials such as paper, photos, magazine clippings or found objects to a flat surface.

Color: Color is an element of design. Eyes see color when light bounces off an object. The four characteristics of color are hue, saturation, value and temperature.

Color wheel: A tool for creating and organizing colors and representing relationships among colors.

Comic: A graphic art form in which images and words are used to tell a story. The images are the main focus and are usually presented in strip or page layout.

Composition: Describes the organization of the elements of design used in an artwork.

Contemporary art: Art created by living artists.

Contour drawing: An outline drawing that characterizes the edge of a form. In "blind" contour drawing, an artist slowly draws each curve on the edges of an object without looking at the paper.

Contour lines: Lines that define the edges, ridges, or outline of a shape or form.

Contrast: A principle of design where light colors are used next to dark colors.

ART GLOSSARY

Cool colors: These are the colors that seem to retreat into the background or distance such as green, blue and purple. Colors often associated with cool places, things or feelings.

Elements of design: Color, line, texture, shape and form.

Focal point: The area in an artwork that attracts the viewer's eye as the center of interest.

Foreground: The part of the picture plane which appears closest to the viewer and in front of other objects. The foreground is often at the bottom of a picture.

Form: An element of design describing a three-dimensional object.

Foreshortening: A technique used in perspective to produce the illusion of an object retreating into the background.

Horizon line: A level line where water or land seems to end and the sky begins.

Hue: Another word for color.

Line: An element of design that is used to define shape, contours and outlines. Different lines can suggest a variety of ideas, movements and moods.

Logo: A visual symbol that identifies a business, club, individual or group.

Middle ground: The part of a picture that seems to be in the middle of the picture plane.

Mixed media: Any artwork which uses more than one medium.

Monochromatic: Made using different shades and tints of one color.

Organic shape: Non-geometric or free-flowing shape.

Perspective: The technique used to represent a three-dimensional world (what we see) on a two-dimensional surface (a piece of paper or canvas) in a way that looks realistic. Perspective is used to generate an illusion of space and depth on a flat surface

Pattern: Lines, colors or shapes repeated in a planned way.

Pointillism: A technique of painting, commonly attributed to Georges Seurat, in which tiny dots of color are placed close together. From a distance, the dots seem to disappear and the colors blend.

ART GLOSSARY

Primary colors: The basic colors—red, blue and yellow—from which all other colors can be mixed.

Secondary colors: The colors produced by mixing equal amounts of any two primary colors: blue and red produce purple, yellow and red make orange, and blue and yellow make green.

Sgraffito: A technique created by scratching into paint to reveal the colors underneath.

Shade: Dark value of a color made by adding black.

Shape: An element of design describing the outer form or outline of an image created using line, value, color and/or texture. Shapes may be geometric or organic, positive or negative.

Sketch: A quick drawing that is used as a reference or plan for an artwork.

Space: An element of design that describes the area around, within or between images or other elements of design.

Still life: An artwork depicting a grouping of inanimate objects.

Subject: A topic or idea represented in an artwork.

Symmetry: Symmetry is demonstrated when portions of the object on opposite sides of a line of symmetry are mirror images one of the other.

Tertiary colors: Colors produced by mixing primary colors with secondary colors.

Tint: Light value of a color made by adding white.

Texture: An element of design describing the surface quality of an object.

Wash: Is created by adding water to paint making it thin enough to allow colors applied underneath to show through.

Warm colors: Warm colors are used to make an object seem to advance into the foreground. Red, yellow and orange are warm colors. They suggest warm places, things and feelings.

Value: The lightness or darkness of a color.

Vanishing point: In linear perspective, a position on the horizon where lines or rays between near and distant places appear to come together.

STUDENT ART CERTIFICATES

SUPER ARTIST

Keep it up!

ARTIST SUPERSTAR!

GREAT ART!

www.ingramcontent.com/pod-product-compliance
Lightning Source LLC
Chambersburg PA
CBHW062345220526
45469CB00008B/2852